LED BY THE NOSE

Also by Jenny Joseph from Souvenir Press

Warning: When I am an Old Woman I Shall Wear Purple

Other books by Jenny Joseph

The Unlooked-for Season
Rose in the Afternoon
The Thinking Heart
Beyond Descartes
Persephone
The Inland Sea
Beached Boats (with Robert Mitchell)
Selected Poems
Ghosts and Other Company
Extended Similes
All the things I see

LED BY THE NOSE

A Garden of Smells

JENNY JOSEPH

SOUVENIR PRESS

First published 2002 by
Souvenir Press Ltd,
43 Great Russell Street, London WC1B 3PD

This paperback edition 2005
Reprinted 2005, 2008

Wood engravings by
Yvonne Skargon
© Yvonne Skargon 2002

ISBN 978 0 285 63695 8

Typeset by Dorchester Typesetting Group Ltd
Printed in Great Britain by Creative Print and Design Group (Wales), Ebbw Vale

To the long-suffering neighbours of my rural slum,
Chick and Charmian Henwood:
brilliant gardeners, very dear friends.

Acknowledgements

This has been a sociable book to prepare and it is a pleasure to thank those many friends and acquaintances who have let me badger them with questions, and joined in the hunt for sensation. I would also like to thank the artist Yvonne Skargon for her work in contributing the marvellous wood engravings to the book.

An extract from *Led by the Nose* was published in the magazine *Proof* edited by Bel Mooney and published by South West Arts in 2000 as a millennium project.

Contents

Introduction

Gardens are often talked of with a view to the colours, shapes, vistas and prospects that will delight the eye. 'With a view to' – precisely. Suggestions in books and gardening tips in newspapers and magazines help us to think in terms of giving a show of colour, of banking flowers in gradations of height to get the best display, of using leaves and space so as to give a foil to the shape or tint of our perfect blooms, of planting to give variety of light and shade, of mass to set off individual specimens, of a succession of colour, especially perhaps in dark corners, so that when the cotoneaster berries are dwindling and the bright beads no longer cheer the gloomy hedge they're set against, the yellow stars of the winter jasmine are ready to catch the brief sunlight of a January frost.

It is only my *intended* garden, of course, that goes like this. In my *actual* garden, things grow and flower if, when and where they will, in the shape and size they – or, at any rate, not I – decide. This happens however much I pore over information on the backs of seed packets about expected height, however much I determine that this year I will do everything at the right time and be more strong-minded and in control.

My pleasure in other people's gardens is different from the joys I get from my own. In other gardens, I stand and gaze gluttonously at the deep herbaceous borders with wonderful clumps stepped back in order of height and bulk, clear good brown soil in between, flowers out at the same time, immense variety of little delights setting each other off in the space beneath; at the rockeries with their delicate rock roses and miniatures, the gravel paths properly edged, the green sweep of grass with the flowering bush or birch tree dripping its fronds, the clumps of daffodils in the grass at just the right distance beyond, towards the wild bit where there is a proper boarded square for different stages of compost set neatly against a wall and overhung with a beautiful spreading beech; poppies where they ought to be for their loud splashes of colour to have full effect, backed by a wall or clump of different taller green; or, at the front of the house with no garden, a stone trough or tub where the pansies don't straggle higher than the wallflowers and each petal glows.

But going into my garden is not like this. Every time, it is a journey of exploration, a voyage of discovery. It is in the mood of enquiry that I wander down my garden path. For I go to find out what has happened, rather than to order what shall be; to wonder what chance has brought it about that this year the peony has opened to a flower and not browned and shrivelled in the bud; to be pleased that the feathery fronds are indeed from the carrot seed I sowed and gave up for lost after the too heavy, too early rains, and not the love-in-a-mist that seeds itself and which I am not ruthless enough with, for it is pretty to have a bit of that scatty blue among the vegetables, and the feathery fronds do not seem rapacious like dock.

Even if I didn't like the taste of rhubarb, I would still grow it for that marvellous moment you get when, stumbling about in a dark day after what seems like weeks of shutting out even the fact that a garden is there at all, you suddenly see these protuberances, these fleshy knobs pushing through the earth. Of course, I put it there once. I decided, once, where it should be, but its appearing again now is still a wonderful surprise. I try to look after or at least appreciate what comes up, like someone who has planned a party but gives in to the circumstances when the guests turn it into something else.

'Being in the garden' therefore is a quite different activity from growing things to give us fine sights as a gardener proper does. I have never understood how anyone can feel they've been to a place by going (and remaining) in a car to look at a view. You must breathe the air of a place to know where you are, and being in your garden is, of course, being in its air and receiving its smells, as well as absorbing its appearance which those with sight can do.

I think many people who enjoy looking at things do also experience them through their noses, but we are far less conscious of what is coming in to us by that sense, and our experience of the world is rarely defined or discussed in terms of smell. I have always felt the battery of the world on my sense of smell as well as on my other senses and have been surprised sometimes that people don't use their noses more. (You cannot, of course, shut your nose as you can your eyes, and an acute or activated sense of smell is not an unmixed blessing.)

I remember going to look at fabrics in a shop with a friend, and she was ashamed of me because, while feeling a particular cloth, I smelt it. The nose is a useful means of information when choosing cloth; but smell is a bit of a taboo subject still.

I think of gardens and the life beyond them in terms of smell. Or rather, my life operates in terms of smell. It is not smell isolated from other sensations, of course. The untrappability and power of odour is that it mingles and moves with everything else on the air, light waves, sound waves, so that it is very enmeshed in one's whole situation.

This book is the result of my habit of operating through as many of my senses as possible. While I hope the book will be of interest to sighted people to remind them of a dimension (possibly overlooked) to their use of and enjoyment of plants, I hope blind people might benefit as well. Even if they haven't got gardens, they might like to hear about plants they could enjoy. By planting a garden with a sense of (not with a view to) what a blind person could enjoy, and therefore take an active part in, I imagine everyone's interest would be enhanced.

Finally, and basically, since the book is based on personal experience, to think that there are different sorts of garden might cheer those who, like myself, are never going to get their garden quite the way they had seen it in the mind's eye. Perhaps if our gardens smell heavenly, it doesn't matter too much if they don't look like the ones in the pictures.

January

There is a young moon. A little light from a street lamp gleams on the ground, for the heavy frost has not weakened all day. It is fresh though still, but not yet brass-monkey freezing. It is rather mysterious in the shadowy garden, coatings of hoar re-ordering the prominence of the outlines, of clump, sack, rubbish, bush, wall and bench.

The leaves are crisp to the foot but, underneath the crackle, the grass they cover is soft and giving, comforting to the feet, almost silkily sliding-soft as I cross my patch of turf to a path in the corner.

The garden smells only of cold, with a whiff from the coal of fires hanging about because of the lack of wind. The frost does not kill the fumes that rise quite strongly from the road whenever a car passes, even though the road is out of sight below my bottom garden wall.

My compost pile near this wall, usually odoriferous to say the least, gives off nothing, even when sniffed close up, not even from recent orange skins. My old manure next to it is indistinguishable, and from a handful of more recent manure not a whiff either. But when I grub around at the bottom of a cage of leaves, the lower layers of which are about three years there, and break off a crumbly handful from the compacted cake, I can tell it is leaf-mould by its smell. It is warm and dry and nice to my hand, and it smells of the woods.

I come back down the path to my back door. Here it is darker, sheltered by hedge and wall and shed. A clump of herb robert I let grow over a rotting log and pile of stones under the yew hedge had flourished late and vigorously in the warm autumn. I bent to where I remembered it had been, put my hand round some soft frail stems, the leaves little dark stipples against the dark, and at once I knew it was the herb robert – that pungent smell that hits you when you are pulling up its loose roots when weeding came with full force across the breathless air. You will not get rid of that rather cat-like acrid smell from your hands without a good wash, and as I went to do that I realized why a friend of mine, noticing the weed that I had let be, had admired the 'pretty little pelargonium'.

If you have had a mild Christmas and only now remember to bring in any pots of geranium you tucked in protected cormers near your back door, as I do, you have only to brush your finger against leaf or stalk, or pick off a dead leaf, and the smell, since there are not others to combat it, is as rank and rife as in hot summer. Not a pleasant smell but if it reminds us of hot sun on stone and gardens of the south, a smell worth releasing into the pure icy air of January.

There were two other things I picked up on my night errand. A couple of bits of sawn old floorboard, from my sawing session earlier in the day when the smell of pine had added to my pleasure in my box of kindling. Wood for the fire gets you warm twice: once when you saw, again when you burn it, and the pleasure to the nose is repeated. For nearly all purposes, including getting the right nasal memories attached to fires in winter, old used wood is best.

When I got in and put my geraniums on the window-sill, I found crumpled in my hand a yellow rose, not dead but translucent, mummified. The last rose of winter, it had stayed on the stem, just visible from my kitchen window when the wind bobbed it that way. Although bought for its scent – 'Golden Showers' – it has not yet fulfilled my expectations for perfuming that corner. I lifted the wan little remainder to my face, cool on my mouth, and as if from far away a faint echo of warmth and the busyness of another season flittered across the air in my kitchen like a ghost.

The first month of the year seems the longest, slowest one. By the time we start it properly, after the gap for New Year's celebrations, daylight is already beginning to stretch, but the days may be cloudy and close, and we are often kept low by winter ills. If, at the end of January, a hard north wind quietens and swings south bringing a thaw, dispersing dank mists so we can see the sky and even the sun, the world is suddenly so full of colour and prettiness and activity that we feel we have taken a great leap into another season in one day.

Things have been happening all the time, of course – growth pushing, light unfurling. Now the buds that had made slight swellings on brittle twigs in December are opening into flower. The winter-flowering shrubs send out some of the strongest and most delicious fragrance of the year. It is as if they need very strong scent to get themselves noticed in cold weather. Chinese witch hazel, its name equally attractive in Latin (*Hamamelis mollis*), and the honeysuckle bush that declares itself to be most fragrant, are among the earliest and therefore most cherished. Their flowers come in advance of their leaves, looking at first glance like excrescences, so the luxury of their smell is even more surprising as we have not been watching leaf buds break in anticipation.

In sheltered places, mahonia might start its long season now. Much used in public gardens, it gives good value of strong perfume free on the air possibly until late spring. Anyone trudging along the bleak underground passage from the tube station at South Kensington in London to visit the Natural History Museum may be uplifted, on emerging into the drizzle of a winter's day, by the shrub's warm heavy scent. An inspired bit of planning! They have planted mahonia bushes alongside the path that goes across a rather wearisome space to the distant entrance.

What we are most eager for are signs of life breaking through the dark cave of winter, pushing up through the ground into the day: snowdrops, the first early crocus, the first of the early irises – *Iris danfordiae*.

We go out to look closely at ground we have forgotten the existence of while we have kept warm inside. We may find snowdrops being lifted by the light above the surface of earth or snow where formerly they were like greeny white crumbs lying on the soil. They don't smell yet, but they will.

Janus, god of exits and entrances, was often figured as a sculpted two-faced head above porticos, one side facing backwards saying goodbye to the old year, the other looking ahead to the next one: god of nostalgia and memory, and equally of hope and anticipation, greeting the new. I think he would be appropriate as a garden god, for that is exactly what happens in a garden. There is nothing of which one can say more truly 'In my end is my beginning' than plants.

If I had a Janus head to set down in time not place, I would position him not on New Year's Eve, but about 18 January. He looks back to the cauled dim days of the winter solstice. The ground is either sodden, or lifeless in the grip of frost. If we have this remission, this break, this volte-face in late January, he will perhaps spy a scrap of pale yellow among a clump of leaves suddenly green where we had seen nothing but dark hedge before – a primrose sheltering under dull twigs, like an eye peeping, a bright slit under a weary eyelid.

A gleam of sun comes through the warp of twigs of the bare hedge, falling across the face of my Janus. It lights up the curve of his finely carved brow, the ridge of his nose and one smooth cheek and nostril. A little breeze makes the sunbeam ripple shadows across it, the nostril flares, tensed with drawing in air.

He is prognosticating not looking forward, my garden Janus, testing the air for smells with his fine enquiring nose. We don't receive much yet but sense fresh life being wafted towards us on the airwaves from the year opening ahead.

February

The smoke of a bonfire is drifting from beyond a wall but I can't smell it. The slow smoke disperses into the air for it is a dank and dim and dripping day. A bus turning in an empty mid-day silence brought me a whiff of diesel. No windless cold seems to cut that off. Apart from that, the phlegm masking the inside of my head seemed to have encumbered the air passages outside it.

There are times up here when it isn't definitely raining but it's as if the air is weeping, drenching, silently. Maybe from the valley, if they are in daylight, we look as if wrapped in cloud but up here it doesn't feel as definite as that: just a cowl of wet dark. No smells are coming through the chill moisture, not even off wet wood and grass or slime or rot. As

I come in from the bottom of my garden, I think this is the time to be in and stay in and shut out the outside world that has shut itself off.

On top of the shoulder-height wall on either side of the path that dips down to my back gate at road level, I had put two plantlings of juniper a friend had given me in autumn. I absent-mindedly passed my hand over it, perhaps to find out if the frond felt alive. Whether they will take I don't know but parts of them are still green. The strong clean smell from my hands at once penetrated the obfuscation of my sinuses. Resinous healthy echo of friendship. Further up the path, a few grey wisps were still on my lavender plants, two cuttings I had put in either side the beginning of the cinder path that backs my vegetable patch. So I picked a bit with the unjunipered hand and the strength of the lavender smell from the grey old needles and the stalk I rubbed was unbelievable from those dowdy bits of twig – such pungence. It remains a favourite through the ages, and itself seems almost everlasting.

Removing the matted remains of Virginian stock and alyssum stems from the edge of a raised bed by my back door to see what had come through under the snow, I uncovered, fresh and viridique, a spray of crisp parsley. No need to crush this and sniff closely. The minute I picked the stem, an invigorating juicy whiff of parsley suffused the air. This bed is really for flowers, but I let parsley grow where it will, as it won't always, and I was rewarded for my 'let-live' habits by feeling more alive, as a deep breath of parsley invigorates me and clears my head as does an inhalation of mint. But I have the snow to thank for it. Fresh-cut bright green parsley on potatoes in darkest February – what luck!

By my back door is a pot with lemon thyme still fresh and green from the autumn. My house is full of lemons, part of daily diet in winter, but the aroma released from this tiny leaf hardly bigger than discs of duckweed as I crumble it on my kitchen table is none the less welcome.

11

The next day, after a morning as closed in as ever, something must have shifted in the upper air, for suddenly there were distances and some weight was lifted from the head. Even a gleam of sun struggled through from above the yew hedge. It shone direct on to the raised sheltered bed by my back door and as if in time to music a sickly white stem of a crocus became a delicate flower lined with lilac. It would have a faint smell, I thought. Crocuses are among our most fragrant flowers. These are early species crocuses, white outer sheath and pale purple inside when open. I dipped my nose as near to the deeply orange stamens as I could and practically staggered back with the scent of honey in my head. The sky drew over, the day closed, the flower shut and disappeared from sight and scent, but there it is, and there they all are, crowding out of the ground, the early crocuses; and the slightest indication from the sun will expand them on to the air.

Only now at the end of February is the month living up to its reputation for filling the ditches. The steady drench all day is just what will bring on the daffodil shoots that seem to double their height daily.

Having bought my Sturon onion sets and some maincrop Desirée potato seed in the pouring rain (Arran Pilot, which I like to put in as a second early, are not so easy to find; they are promised for 'next week'), I went into my loft, which gets plenty of light, to spread out my purchases. I traced at last the sweetish 'quite pleasant smell' visitors had detected up there at Christmas. After dismissing the possibility that it might be visitors' socks, or a Christmas cake which I'd kept up there, and having sorted out a bag of rather strong-smelling potatoes (not mine but bought from a farm in wet December) I had decided it was nothing that needed pursuing. It was not the smell of rotting plaster or dry rot or the forgotten remnants of a midnight feast. But now I found a box of apples collected from a friend's garden in autumn, none rotting, reminding me that if I have time there are still enough left to make some more apple ginger jam. The smell of jam-making had percolated the whole house when I made some before Christmas. Now added to the air in the loft above the more earthy smell of the seed potatoes is the duct-clearing odour of onions.

This is a good time, if you can't get on with anything else, to look in boxes and bags where you've put produce, roots, bulbs or corms and see what's happening to them. I found five hyacinths, each with a tough triangle of light green, on a shelf in my shed, put on one side for something I'd neglected to do in the autumn. I quickly shoved them into a strip of earth by the path where later they will, I hope, perfume the air to maximum benefit and halt me on my way to some job further down the garden. With the protecting moist, drinking earth at last round their shrivelled papery dried out skins I felt less dry and shrivelled myself.

Early next morning the roads, paths, air were still suffused with damp but as a gleam of sun flickered through, the sky suddenly lifted. I went out to see what a pale streak was, in the bed by the back door, seen through the steam of the bathroom window. Some tiny cream crocuses that I had forgotten I'd put in had come through and a few yellow ones were emerging too but they, like everyone but the early birds, knew it was too soon in the day to open yet and they don't release their smell when shut. The air smelt freshly with the damp but with that invigorating feel when it is drying up, not the sense of clammy shut-in blotting out when it's going to shroud everything all day.

Later, when the light was stronger, the clump of lavender-coloured species crocus sprang open like a chorus exactly on cue. They opened their star shapes all at once for me to bury my face in their cool delicacy and inhale their honey; to get the benefit of the snowdrops I still have to bend down to them and turn them up for me to sniff close – worth it every time – although I'm sure their fragrance is being released into the air just above ground level for the insects. One would need to be a

Lilliputian, or a Tom Thumb, and lie on one's back under their delicate canopies, as we might under a lilac tree, but that is far ahead yet.

What is here and very much now, though, is one of the best smells of the year – sarcococca; sarcococca that keeps its glossy green leaves all the year. We have waited impatiently looking at those buds so full of promise since early January for their prolific sweet fragrance to perfume the air. Two people I know with sarcococcae have planted them either side of the entrance to their house. Someone coming up to such a door with bad intent might be more turned from it by the sarcococca's perfume than by notices of burglar alarms, and anyone leaving the house must feel accompanied by good will. Another bush whose delicious scent is released this month flowers on its bare stem. There is no gradual cladding and bulking out of the plant with leaves, but sudden glory from nakedness: the earliest of the daphnes – *Daphne mezereum*.

March

March is certainly coming in like a lion – a roaring beast up here. After the gale had torn wider and wider the covering to the sky to let the blue in, it was a bright sunny enticing outside world. Dry, perfect for getting on with all the jobs I'm in the middle of, digging a trench for peas, smelling the ground, clearing, burning, some sowing at last, too, perhaps; and would not all this movement in the air carry perfumes?

Not a bit of it. I don't even get fully out of the back door when I am back in like a shot. I am obviously the creature the lion is after. It is a killing wind, not the 'gentle gales' of the songs, wings laden with balm. This ill wind does me no good. It brings ailments, and probably illness. I will not be able to do a thing.

I make a sally to my shed, fill some pots and boxes with fine compost and scuttle back to the house. And there, all over the matting on
my hall floor, I spread my packets and envelopes of seeds, tins with
some saved from last year, paper bags – the result of impulse-buying in
Woolworth's one wet day last week and, finally, my list of things to get
and do. I am as happy as on a wet Sunday, giving up the battle against
the weather, indulging myself warm and safe inside with thoughts of
heat and balmy evenings outside later.

I put into pots different varieties of sweet pea seed (all of them said
to be fragrant), seed of Little Gem lettuce, which will only smell of green
freshness, and antirrhinum, aquilegia, penstemon. Then I spread a plastic sheet on a board under my loft window and put the lot up there, for
I have no greenhouse, and the loft begins to smell more of earth than
ever.

In the evening I had occasion to go down into the valley and as I
came back up in the dark in the icy air, the wind seemed not so wild.
The air was lighted by a sharp young moon and the sky was thickly
strewn with clear stars, Orion still marching across as if pursuing, rather
than pursued by, the winds. The air was too keen to do anything. It hurt
the inside of my nose so none of the smells I'm sure it bore got to me.
The next day I felt proved right about not sowing seed outdoors too
early. The cars going early to work were coated with white and making
tracks on snowed-over roads. Then more snow came horizontally past
my window. The street I live on runs east–west and that was the direction of the wind. On such days in my mind's eye, where the bend in the
road eastward ends my view down it, there begin to stretch the snow
fields of Siberia.

There is nothing to smell but cold and coal dust and some sharp
fumes as I stoke up the fire. And then the snow stops, and later it melts.
The wind returns but I find myself outside, spending far too long in a

sheltered corner between wall and shed disentangling my clematis. Jade-green leaves have begun budding at the nodes of these wiry crinkly-brown tangled strands of twine. I should cut through the whole Gordian knot at its base, stake up a firm support and be done in fifteen minutes. But at least there was no one else there to get annoyed at my untwining and clipping as people do when they bring scissors when I'm untying a parcel and tell me sternly to stop wasting time. There were only stones falling on me, the clematis and the bed it is in, from a neighbour's rotten neglected wall. Now I have long straggly budding tendrils already making towards the top of the shed which this year it ought to cover.

When I straightened up from my absorption just before dusk, I spied furled striped leaves of miniature tulips emerging, a little swell of yellow in a green clump of primrose leaves, and the leaves of the honeysuckle plant on the other side of the shed, which will surely this year flower, and reach up to meet the cascading clematis. What a mingling that will be if . . . My fingers are by now numb and hurting with the bite in the air as the day shuts down and although there are, to me just now, no smells on the air, yet it is true that spring is in the air, for that edge, that stirring, that restlessness, that waywardness – that is spring.

And where is the little lamb that is meant to trot gently in the wild paw prints of the lion? March is going out but the winds are sweeping clean, clearing the passages, bringing air to be sure, but no soft stirrings that give you a chance to appreciate the savours it brings. Everything is moving: a little cypress I see from my back window seems to be swaying to the jazz I have on the radio; everything is stirring, hit and miss. Whatever dust and dirt you sweep up is blown straight back at you again. It's a hard fight but we can't go back now. On over, says the wind. The birds are active. Are the chaffinches, I wonder, pecking at my buds?

Such scents as come from flowers still have to be bent for. The later snowdrops (Allens are among the scented ones) seem to have the stronger smell. The perfume of my snowdrops has given good value this year. The honey of my early crocus which caught me at a corner when the sun opened them has gone by now but the fatter goblets of purple, then yellow, then white that succeeded them provide deep draughts of sweetness when I nose into them, the purple the strongest.

Everything now gives way to daffodils. I am a bit one-sided about daffodils. If I were allowed one sort of flower only on my desert island it would have to be daffodils. When nothing was out in a flat in-between time earlier in the month, I came home from a tiring visit to find a bunch of cut daffodils in my letter box. Some telepathy from my neighbour had moved her to this inspired act. I retired to bed for a couple of days, downed by the slight attack of plague that had been dogging me throughout the month, brought a jug of lemon and the daffodils up from the kitchen window-sill where I had set them, and together they effected the cure. What crisp fragrance, what unburdensome vigour comes from leaning one's fevered brow to the cool touch of those extraordinary trumpet tubes, and what health one breathes in from their stringent breath.

If there is one smell of spring it is the smell of daffodils, not the sweeter, further-travelling, sometimes over-powering jonquil which comes later when the sun is stronger, nor quite the very elusive smell of the small wild daffodils which no doubt have been out in their profusion in the churchyards, banks and the meadows round Newent and Dymock and Kempsey towards Wales, while I have been shut up here. These are the same sort as the star-like crowds that Wordsworth came on by the lakes two hundred years ago. No, it is your ordinary all-yellow single trumpet that catches the wind in its strong fragrant horn and almost rings the bell for spring. They must be out in the parks in London now, I think, while we crouch indoors in this wet weather, and they may be blowing in the sheltered places in the valley, but mine up here are shut like me, though, unlike me, swelling with promise, their good humour not destroyed by the winds as mine is.

When the wind became mild and wet instead of wild and wet, I went out to see what was coming up and all seemed disappointment. The primrose in bud had a few rags of pale petal beside it – some bird had pounced on the one bold enough to open, and torn it up. My neighbour has a lovely cluster in a sheltered place and they open to the west light but I receive as yet no fragrance through the hedge.

There are all sorts of things 'in waiting' even if it does feel as if there is no reason for the year's clock, stopped under the hard wind, to get going again. Bending down close to the tips of hyacinths sheathed and closed, strong green and full of juice and promise, I was surprised to get a whiff of sweet scent. My imagination or my sense of smell was even stronger then, than even I had thought – and then I realized that the scarf I had swathed round my head had come untucked and an end had blown across my face and it retained the scent it had absorbed from being in a drawer with an old scent bottle.

By the end of the month, although the cold and grey continued, there was a glint of night blue from the long grass round my apple tree – *Iris reticulata*, like a bright eye flashing through long lashes; no scent from them in this cold. I planted them under the influence of the ending of Leonard Woolf's *Downhill all the Way* which moves me every time I read it. One or two of the broad beans sown in November seem to have survived the winter and are pushing through the dead leaves I covered them with before the snow came to give them a further layer of protection.

Once you brave what looks and feels like winter, there are, after all, things happening: my delphinium (blue) and phlox (white, I hope, as the white flowers, particularly with the phlox, generally have the stronger scent) are sprouting, and at last one daffodil bud is about to break, the yellow petticoat to its green top skirt showing through, a yellow cut like the slashed sleeves of the Elizabethans with undersilk bulging out. At the bottom of their slender strip-like leaves, under a crystal drop of water, the grape hyacinth bud is blueing – what promise of fragrance there! My cream crocuses, the first year I've had them, have stayed out a long time, and now tulip tips are coming through the soil. My rhubarb is, at last, coming through. I had been expecting it earlier. I think it will flourish this year as it has sat for months under a thick cladding of manure lavished on it in the autumn. Whenever it appears, expected or not, it is such an extraordinary thing to see, that rude red knob containing shoot and leaves and expectation of such taste, that it is always a thrill of pleasure.

I did plant one thing. I was given some snowdrops, a sort different from those giving so much outside my back door. If you want to move snowdrops, you must do so while they are still in flower or at least leaf, for you mustn't let the bulbs dry out. As a most suitable last act in this battling setting-back month, as a defiant gesture against the weather gods, I put them still flowering in three groups under my apple tree at the bottom of the garden where next year they will mingle with the *Iris reticulata*.

April

If daffodils are the smell of spring, the smell that signifies the beginning of spring activity for humans hit me when March was giving way to what seemed likely to be the usual wintry April.

They kept saying apologetically on the radio 'not very spring-like weather, I'm afraid' to which I wanted to answer that it was indeed spring-like, that spring is always a hard time, cold and rattly and wet, a time when more old people die than in the winter since they have not the resources left to cope with the demands that the growing season makes on them. Anyone who plans to go away at Easter deserves what they get, thought I, and didn't they remember ('they' were my family by now) the year when the two who had gone camping actually came back

in the middle of the four-day reprieve, not because dysentery had swept the company or their tents had blown off the cliff, or the cliff had been washed into the sea, but because it had been just too cold even for them, and that they came back dripping and depressed in the middle of Sunday afternoon to find the rest of us, who had been going to paint the sitting-room, playing Monopoly by the fire, no seasonal cleaning or painting contemplated and nothing in the larder. This, after all, is the time of year for which the wise made sure of their stocks of wood and coal in the autumn; this the season against which one puts fruit by in freezers and bottles, this the time when we see the point of the thrift that has ensured that the knee-warming liquor saved from Christmas largesse has not been used on frivolous absent-minded social occasions, but kept for times of serious medicinal need.

Travelling west down the motorway one dark pouring day when things were still like that, I smelt, even with the windows up, the smell of cut grass. Was it my imagination, was it perhaps petrol mixed with rain, something from a passing car? I lowered the window and in with the damp air and the flap of the gale flooded the sweet freshness of grass, the unmistakable smell that, like a bell, chimes for a new season: wet cut grass mixed with petrol. A week later the juices of growth were being wafted on the air all over the county, together with the buzz of the busy human insects' machines as a spring such as we have not known for years emerged from the doldrums. There we were basking in the sun, up and out at bright 6 am, still clearing and planting and pottering and potting, and bonfiring and edging and raking, as dusk drove us stumbling in, surprised to find it was nine o'clock, and not five in the afternoon.

The flowers that had come out in the sheltered places on banks and in woods – violets and primroses kept fresh by the rain at the beginning of the month – had been too shy and careful to part with much of their

22

scent. Now they opened to the sun, and woods and walks began to have a lighter sweeter air. The air began to be a mingling of fragrances.

A strong strand in the weave by this time is my vigorous daffodils, like freshly washed cotton in the sun as I go down the path. The hyacinths and then the muskier grape hyacinths are really the first flowers whose scent is free on the air after the early crocus, perhaps because they come out when the air is warmer. For me, the smell of hyacinths is pre-eminent, as one might say that the lion is a king among beasts. They stand so crisp and curly, like the ringlets of a cascading head of shining hair in fine condition on a beautiful head of good posture. I like the blue ones best and the white. The pink ones are all right, but I would not have a yellow hyacinth. To me, that is like blue cake – unpalatable. Some people, I know, find their scent too overwhelming, but I am prepared to be overwhelmed and will inhale it until I'm dizzy, but you can keep away from it and it will still fill the air with heady sweetness. It is much stronger than anything else in my garden at this time; the other flowers that smell – daffodils, pansies, primroses, cowslips, cultivated primulas, early iris – have still to be sniffed close to be appreciated and some, like forget-me-not, beginning now to blur my flower-beds with blue, only smell because, knowing they're meant to, I try to find a smell.

One plant with a very distinctive smell that may still have been out up to now in some gardens is stinking hellebore. I do not find it a stink but a good smell. I put three seedlings in at the beginning of April, looking forward to their stink through the winter and spring next year when other smells are faint. I was given the flowers of the plant from which my seedlings came and their cream bell-like heads, petals tipped with dried-blood red, hung down from a little pot on my window-sill for weeks before fading. The warmth of the room no doubt brought out the smell more than the outside air would have done.

Before and during and after the short stunning apogee of the hyacinth, there is the wallflower, and once you remember the wall-flower you realize that it must have pride of place in its turn – and it is a long turn. At one spot by my path, there is a yellow wallflower from last year grown now almost to bush proportions: my favourites are the velvet-brown and I would not want mauve. As it came out, a fine daffodil by it was still in scent, and underneath it were grape hyacinths, muscari – well-named, for their scent is huskier than the more flamboyant cousin. In the same strip by the path, pansies open fully to the sun. Especially pleasing to me is an unusual dwarf iris given to me as an exotic present which did not flower last year. Now a fat sheath bulges with a slash of dark silk in it.

By the middle of the month, just when I'd ordered some more coal in case of shivers in May, the sun was like a conductor drawing out the full orchestra, all playing strongly together. The bees were bumbling around and although I've been told it's the colour of the aubrieta they go for, when the hot sun is on mine I seemed to smell a delicate honey which surely attracts the insects. Weeding, I caught a sweet whiff and there was nothing else open nearby. The carpet of forget-me-not that I let grow where it will until I want the space next month, now does add its light scent to the air in the hot afternoon. My lilies-of-the-valley promise fair, the pinky-brown tips having elongated into fresh pale green sheaths, but they are as yet an imagined smell and nothing prepares one for the heavenly sweetness when the small mob-cap bells hang open next month.

Every now and then these days as I kneel to sniff a plant or lean my hand on the earth to reach a weed, I think I can smell someone preparing dinner. I must have stepped or leant on one of the almost invisible black needles that turn into the purple-to-green shoots of the *Allium moly*. A healthy clean onion smell, said to keep insects off other plants like roses, they tend to take over your garden, but are good value (if you like the smell of onions) being interesting at every stage from the black needles through purple, to straps of papery seed heads. At least you can always tell where they are as this cultivar of the wild garlic gives off its pungency at every stage. Don't try to use it in the kitchen though, nor the wild garlic which is also making its presence known now in the woods. Chives, after all, are growing at this time, and I have still some leeks to clear which did not grow very big last autumn and are handy for soup when I have come to the end of my last year's stock of that basic culinary bulb. My March-sown onion sets are sprouting nicely with all the rain we've had.

Honeysuckle is twining across the yew hedge into my neighbour's yard. Planted with the 'Golden Showers' rose outside my back door against the only bit of red brick wall for miles, it is getting vigorous, but it was vigorous and healthy last year and still didn't flower. Maybe this year . . . In spite of early and devoted spraying, the rose already shows the black spot that was quite bad last year, so there is a smell of chemical first thing one still morning before the sun we are beginning to take for granted gets on it. First thing also, because it is a job I dislike so want to get it over with.

The leaves on the apple tree are breaking. The great beech bank in the sky on the other side of the road that runs at the bottom of our gardens is suddenly blurred and filling in with bud break. Only a day or two ago the trees were making separate interesting dark outlines of branches and tracery of twigs as they swayed in the gales.

Lilac is coming out – going past a neighbour's garage there was suddenly a lovely ungarage-like smell: I was under a lilac already sending its scent out on the air. Mine – a pale lilac colour, growing above my back gate like a sentinel – is in bud. The only smell I've had from it so far has been the smell from sappy new twig when, last month, I cut off the growth shooting up round its base, to direct the strength into the flower. On the other side of my gate, to hang more sweetness above the passers-by, the philadelphus I planted last autumn looks quite healthy. Its stems have survived snow and wall-mending and it is budding.

My currant bushes and gooseberry are flowering. The blackcurrant is the savour I like the best and if you so much as touch the stem even in winter, let alone the leaf in early spring, you release that strong fruity smell with a tinge of wet iron to it. When ripe, the redcurrant is the most astoundingly delicately beautiful one of them all. Especially with a shaft of sun lighting up the translucency of its cluster of beads, it is almost too pretty to pick and eat, but the ribes, flowering currant, soon to come into its glory round here, I find smells a little too like cats for my pleasure. One is pleased to see anything out and blossoming but if I am truthful, I find it an acquired smell. I decided not to have one in my garden.

And in all this fine weather, prior to giving my grass a tarwash to try to discourage the moss (tarwash, along with Jeyes Fluid, is a smell I find most refreshing), I borrowed my neighbour's superb electric mower. Emptying the box, I was transported back across the years to another garden, the garden I grew up in, to a flat, unshaded lawn where we emptied the box for my father's ritual of mowing the grass. The slaves were not allowed to touch the machinery and, anyway, we never could have got the stripes straight – I can't now. When he was away, we used the hand mower. The grand one had a petrol engine. There was always a little trouble starting it, rather like an outboard on a dinghy, I seem to remember, and we had to hurry in case it rained, so I think the memory of the essential petrol ingredient mingling with the essence of grass juice must have come from there. The pungent smell pricked one's eyes, the bits stuck to the hand, itching it, the insects itched the rest of your body and, later, there was the musty and ammoniac smell of the pile of cuttings and the damp heat in the centre of the pile if you pushed your arm in to test how hay boxes worked. And, yes, it was surprisingly hot.

It seems right to me that the background smell to the life of gardens through half the year should be the smell of grass, for grass is the most basic and most serviceable, most adaptable of all plants. The idea that 'all flesh is grass' is to me an optimistic one.

Easter is the time for outings, and one afternoon with the sun gentle on the greening hedges and the clouds moving off to widen out the sky, we set off to the more open rolling countryside where the soil becomes increasingly red. Hawthorn was beginning to break here and there and the opening beech leaves were that delicate jade-green they only keep for a few days – a translucent and a jade quite different from the later brighter green and a softness as of very young skin to the lips. You get it best if you stand under the tree and look up into the light, perhaps the leaves on a low branch near enough to pull down to brush against your face, enough to bring saliva to your mouth.

When I was expecting a visitor at the end of April, I determined I would not say, 'Oh, if only you had come last week when all the daffodils were out, when it was warm and sunny and fresh and fizzy with spring.' The exceptional heat had drawn out the unwary, and the garden's daffodils, normally such stayers, were short-lived this year; hyacinths were going over rapidly although grape hyacinths still gave the sweetness with an edge to it that haunts the air in the evening by my back door. Narcissi and jonquil, at strategic corners, having opened later, were still fresh and giving freely, and my large tulips newly opened have succeeded to some cheerful dwarf red ones.

I was given some pretty star-shaped Turkana tulips earlier in the year and those are known to have fragrance. What surprises me is that, for some people apparently, tulips do not smell. Once mine open to the sun so that you can get your nose in (making sure there is no insect there before you) there is to my mind (or nose) a heavenly smell. It has a hint of astringency to it, much less sweet than the jonquils. I think I have at last traced what it reminds me of, this afterwaft of spiciness that you get from some peonies, also: it is the smell of slippery elm cooking – slippery elm, that old-fashioned soother made from the inner bark of the North American red elm. Of course, I had no idea what it was when I first smelled it only that I liked the name and loved the smell.

I made a visit to a friend's garden just in time to catch the last heady scent of her *Magnolia stellata* – the heat had brought it out but also exhausted the blossom. I still have not planted the magnolia I promised myself I would have if, one day, I had a garden right for it.

The primroses in shady places are still going strong, or still going delicately. I have one clump under the edge of a privet hedge where one or two of the wild strawberries that bud so early and continue to bear fruit sometimes even into November are beginning to flower. The primroses are now giving out their very delicate fragrance to the air, although I still kneel to bury my face in them, especially when the dews and damps of evening ease it out of them after the heat of the day. Their scent is mingling with the strengthening smell from the pansies that are opening their eyes everywhere. I have them edging my vegetable patch, and they don't always stay on the edge. The fragrance of the wallflowers continues like an uninterrupted strong accompaniment at all times of day, and the pear blossom from the garden west of mine drifts petals across that settle on the grass under my apple tree where the leaf is breaking. Do I smell in that vigorous green the tartness of juicy apples? Probably not, but the leaves do smell fresh and sappy and sharp.

There were two things that my visitor came just at the right time to enjoy the fullness of: the bluebells, succeeding their posher cultivar, the hyacinth, have come into their own, hazing the glades in the woods with blue, and the cherry blossom has burst upon us.

One evening that hadn't quite made up its mind whether to turn its spitting to a drench, or clear up and smile, we walked down into the densely wooded valley to the south of the ridge my house is on. The rain stopped, cool sun slanted on the delicate green of early beech and the pinky-brown of the new copper beech leaves, the colour of a young black cat's ear seen against a strong light. The rain had brought out all the earthy leafy smell of the mould on the wood's floor, and the dark green smell of water and water-weeds and moss by the disused mill-race. Along the tracks in the woods there was the pervading, and to me refreshing, smell of the wild garlic whose starry flowers were beginning to show. As everywhere round here on this porous chalk, after the rain there was the busy sound of water running under the ground, and in some banks a sort of murmuring. We came to a small overgrown garden in front of a cottage with boarded-up windows, the back of which was being used as a workshop. Over the porch a cotoneaster was spreading and to the left a young apple tree was in blossom. By the railings, the grass grew as tall as wheat with a bluebell or two here and there. Then we saw and smelt them everywhere. On the other side of a full ditch where I could not reach them, shone the biggest most perfect clump of kingcups I have seen.

We came back full of soft air, of greenery, of moisture and sappy essences of the things nourished in the protection of those shady streams, much later than we had intended; we came back under breaking buds of beech and lime through my gate in the wall, past clumps of light green leaf of day lilies, roses in leaf, past a place where a hop root I had set in the hopes it would cover a shed was shooting nicely – promise of later delights when spring would be over. You have to remind yourself of these for as the astounding cloud of cherry loosens before the winds which we nearly always get as soon as the blossom of the pink cherry is full on the bough, going through a metamorphosis into brown litter in the gutter as rapid as Cinderella's ballgown into rags, and the daffodils' crisp edges curl and shrink and brown, it is easy to think that with the spring flowers gone and the trees clothed, the most delicious time of year is over.

When visitors depart, it is sometimes difficult to return immediately to routine or get back to work. When I first tried to make jam, the only time I knew I would not be interrupted was after eleven o'clock at night, and I find I still leave jam-making to the small hours. The kitchen was beginning to smell sickly from the bowls of cut rhubarb soaking in sugar that I'd done nothing about for two days – perhaps it would soon only be fit for wine. So late that night, I made the first jam of the year: rhubarb and ginger, and through every pore of the house, blustered around with windy cold, with a third of the year gone, there percolated the warm toffeeish fruity smell of rhubarb, sugar, lemon and ginger. The sweet savour of my husbandry must have reached the gods, for the next day, after exactly a week of cloudy cold weather following our earlier heat-wave, clear skies, hot sun and balmy air returned.

May

Now the year is getting complicated. I am still trying to catch up on putting in seed that could have gone in in March had it not been so wet and cold, and should have gone in in April had it not been so hot and busy catching up on March; but I'm gathering as well. Two things I pick encourage one's efforts to sow and plant, and provide to me the most heartening smells – one might say the sweet smell of success: rhubarb and spring greens. The minute you part the great umbrellas of leaves to get your hand to the bottom of the rhubarb stalk to pull, it gives off its sharp fruity smell, and cutting the early cabbage instead of pulling means you will get a second sprouting from the stalk.

My 'Flower of Spring' cabbage plants set out early last autumn wintered-over well. They seemed to like the snow. The juicy green smell released when you cut the stem is even better when you're cutting up the leaves on the table for the pot. As they're cooking (only enough boiling water to stop the bottom of the pan from burning and a quick stir of the leaves in the heat with the knife), the smell is stronger with a hint of iron in it; this is the strong taste that small children dislike about dark green cabbage leaves. The tender light green stalks are almost the best bit. There's too much taste to need salt. From garden to plate can take less than ten minutes. With a piece of cheddar among the steaming leaves, this is one of the first culinary delights of the year, savour to nose and palate all the way.

Now my small yellow tulips are beginning to open. They will go on into June after the huge red and yellow ones that still smell so musky cease to close in the evening and then finally flop and drop away, little bits of silky rag found in corners far from their stalks. Broom is out on sheltered embankments. The pink and white variegated sort smells sweet, but I like the plain yellow broom best. Cowslip and primula still add their sweetness to the air shaded near the ground. I realized that my lilac was at last breaking into bud when we had some more winds that knocked out the cherry and pear blossom. There were a few clusters of tight lilac buds on the path by my gate. They did not open in water in the house so were wasted by the vandal wind that only plucks to throw away. Berberis is out, japonica and early iris breaking and, one of the best moments, the apple blossom breaking. I have one flower open in its perfection just where I can walk straight up to it and smell it without bending or stretching, and an appley tang does linger after the sweetness.

In sheltered places there are still cherry trees that are a great cloud-puff of almond-scented blossom, and jonquils continue to release their heady sweetness on the air. The strange snakeskin of some fritillaries that were out in my bed by my crocuses has gone dingy and is going over, but there are still grape hyacinths which have an infinitely preferable smell. The needles of the lavender are freshening, mint and chives growing and the broad beans I sowed in the autumn look sturdy. Leaning to admire and weed them, I almost accidentally crushed a leaf and the smell transferred me to the kitchen, putting out dinner on a warm summer evening, it was so beany. But there's many a (black)fly twixt beanflower and beanfeast. If they survive the winter, the broad beans sowed in November are less likely to be molested by blackfly than the spring-sown ones.

One of the year's main pleasures is now beginning its extended influence over the air in the garden: the scent of the Brompton Stocks. Other scents of that heaven-transporting genus are as yet in embryo: some Ten Week stock I sowed has germinated quickly and through this month I scatter seeds of night-scented stock here and there in beds bordering paths. There are already some seeded from last year showing through, together with the lower Virginian stock and the tiny pointed leaves of alyssum. Yellow alyssum, the perennial, has been already perfuming some sheltered walls in sunny corners. I like the low white alyssum. It germinates very easily, seeds itself from year to year, provides about the most breathtaking heavenly honey smell there is to the whole air early and late, and continues beyond autumn. It is pure honey: not too cloying, and if you have no garden and not even a back-door step, if you're high up in a box in a concrete jungle without a balcony, put a box of alyssum on a window-sill (if you have a window-sill, that is) and you'll be all right even on those arid sultry August nights.

But although wistaria is beginning to clad a porch I pass on a walk, and my neighbour's delightful early clematis is hanging its narrow bells through a trellis into my garden, although the lime leaves have emerged from the long slender red buds together with the beech leaves filling in the woods, and the wisps of ash flower herald the breaking of those latest of trees to leaf (and latest to fall in autumn), although the woods are blue and sweet with bluebells, and redolent with wild garlic, and wallflowers are continuing in full scent and my nicotiana seeds have germinated (and been enjoyed by slugs, blast them), and the shallots are shooting up their clusters of juicy pipes and the onion bed is a mass of green points, my alyssum (which I sow direct into the ground in May rather than in boxes inside earlier) is as yet an imaginary pleasure.

I stand in the hot sun with the packet in my hand and look at the pots of germinated sweet pea seedlings I shall soon plant out. I take pleasure also in the buds of the day lilies which have risen on their stalks out of their dense clump of light green strap leaves, the ones on the clump in the sunniest place beginning to show a yellow tinge of what is within; I breathe in the warm pleasant air and think 'Ah, heavenly summer' . . . and the next day I have retreated to my living-room, lit my boiler again, shut the windows and returned to winter. May can indeed be a complicating month.

I am watching my broad bean flowers, which don't seem yet to be blackfly-infested enough to spray. I would much rather not spray if there are enough ladybirds, which feast on the fly, but some winters the cold cuts the ladybird population. When the little broad bean pod forms from the black screw of withered flower low down on the stems, you can pinch out the top flower which is the main locus for the blackfly. My flowers are as yet only in bud but the stalk and leaves smell of that delicious pulse. For the heady smell of the flowers to waft across the air I must wait for the heat of summer.

Meanwhile, in the hedges the wild marjoram is prolific. Last year I made my customary visit to a favourite meadow by the canal, much churned up into crests and hollows of hoof prints by cattle and horses round hummocks covered with blackberry bushes. In this spot grew clumps of flourishing marjoram and many other wild flowers. The canal smell and the sun on the herbage and brambles used to mingle to a drowse, stretching hot mid-day through endless afternoons. But the ground had been churned by JCBs, the hillocks shorn of leafage and it was all bare earth, combed and flattened, the meadow stricken and mucked up. I have never been back there since to see what they built, but I have some marjoram by my path. The plants set to cover things – hop and honeysuckle – are beginning to creep and expand into leaf. It is not their scent, though, that wafts from the corner of the shed I hope they will cover, but the lovely astringent tarwash I have put down in an attempt to control moss in my – should I, dare I say? – lawn.

Nothing has stopped the blackspot but in spite of it my yellow rose is budding. The cold is keeping the peony whose healthy buds excited me last month obstinately shut for a long time, but how sensible to wait.

My day lilies look prolific. They, too, are shut against the cold but the buds are changing shape and getting ready. Lilies have always seemed to me very exotic flowers, special hothouse plants from abroad, but they don't seem to mind the cold, although some come from hot countries: alstroemeria, for instance, the Peruvian lily. I have a clump whose squiggly chinesey-looking sprays of grey-green leaves have come up abundantly again. Their flame will succeed the buttery-yellow of the strongly fragrant day lily. All aspects of them seem to me mysterious. Their roots go down and down. They seem impossible to propagate from division. They disappear utterly, you think you have lost them (growing through to the other side of the world?) and then, suddenly, there the stems are, twisting their curly leaves up into the air. Of course, there are cold parts of Peru. I am always surprised that the delicate almond and the gorgeous magnolia, from the East, are among the first trees to flower in cold London springs, but many plants that we think 'natural' to England were introduced from other climates. If it is not so hot when the day lilies do open, they will last the longer.

My miniature iris that had such a plump bud has opened into three inky purple elegant fleur-de-lys-shaped flowers. They are by the path in the open where, when the sun shines, there is hot sun and a most delicate spicy tang is mingled in their smell, like expensive sweets. But, of course, iris is orris: orrisroot, orris-powder. Is it used in confectionery – in Turkey? It smells as if it is.

Now, at the end of May, the daffodils in the banks by the roads have given way to cow parsley, and the cherry blossom on corners to hawthorn. As a child, I always thought that line of Walter de la Mare's 'and a bush in a corner of May' meant a corner of the month. I had left the commas out. But the tree does have its special place in the month, as it does in so many legends and magical tales. I think the superstitions that have grown up around the ill-luck that results from bringing certain plants into the house have, in the case of the hawthorn, a very practical base. The scent is so strong when branches of the blossom are shut up in a room it can make people feel ill. It needs the open air of the green meadows to absorb it. Cow parlsey in stale air, or sniffed too close, can have an unpleasant after-odour that you do not expect from its delicate lacy flower-head.

I am longing to put out some of the plants that you need to keep inside 'until there is no fear of frost'. When it is baking and hot here on our garden backs which stretch southward, you feel summer has come, that the endless sun in the great clear sky is going to reign with no interruption for weeks, but the temperatures can drop 20 degrees in a night and one morning in mid-May the sun sparkling on the grass had not melted the furred coat of frost on my shed roof by nine o'clock.

That felt roof which I see from the warmth of my bathroom is one of my weather tests. The other, for wind, is the beech hedge with lilac and laburnum trees above it across the road in front, which looks north. It may be calm and gentle in the house and at the sheltered back even, while the foliage across the road and the shoots of the 'Albertine' rose beginning to clad the railing opposite may be tossing about like mad.

So with the cold battering winds and the possibility of frost, it's not the time to put out tomatoes or my dahlias which started to sprout and look healthy under the April sun's influence and are now shooting up too quickly. One of them is growing like a tree and reminds me of the Ionesco play about the body that outgrew the house it was left in, or Alice in Wonderland when she grew too big with her head pressed against the ceiling. I probably started them off too early or, having no greenhouse, put them in a place where they had to stretch for the light.

They must now share my deep kitchen window-sill crowded with other things that need to be in the light but not in the wind: the one morning glory that germinated from seeds sown last month, and a box of assorted spray chrysanthemum cuttings that would like this wind no more than I do but need to go into the proper earth; and the various sizes of pots of geraniums that have been in flower for some time now, rewarding my efforts of putting them out in the sun on warm days and remembering to bring them in at night. It is the chrysanthemum leaves I delight to smell now as, with relief, I clear my steamy cluttered window-sill into the sunny yard at midday. The plants and I and the house need air after the shut-in days. It is rather like getting invalids out into the air or at least downstairs and having a good go at clearing up and airing their rooms.

Although I accept the stink of geranium leaves as a sign of unique-ness and vigour and am pleased to have some in pots because they remind me of Cornwall and the Mediterranean, it is the odour of chrysanthemuns I love. The merest brush of a finger on one of the leaves will set it off, and what refreshment in damp curtailed autumn days will the tangle of their sprays of bloom give if I treat them carefully now.

I have put my sweet pea seedlings in the ground under the trellis that is the boundary instead of a wall between my neighbour and me. The seed sown earlier in the ground doesn't seem to have been very successful – perhaps here there are too many insects, little animals and birds for whom the early shoots are a find when nothing much else so nourishing is about, but they germinate and grow well enough sown in pots of compost in the yard in March and April. Until their and my enemies chew through their tender stalks, I can imagine the trellis full of butterfly fragrance along the path, continuing all summer and even beyond autumn if you pick the blooms before they go to seed.

My kitchen table is full of dreams, delights in embryo, seed packets of things that can go straight in the ground now, seeds that could only be started in pots inside earlier – marrows, sunflowers, alyssum, asters, but our actual sweets are a few last daffodils in places that were sheltered from the hot sun we had at Easter, cherry blossom that here and there has survived the winds, the apple blossom strengthening, and the tulips – perhaps their scent is a bit like apple, not spicey, after all, or is that only the cluster near my apple tree?

The pansies too are increasing everywhere, and added to their scent when the sun is on them is a faint smell from the strawberries now coming nicely into flower. The wild ones have a different scent, if you can tell difference in a whiff so elusive. The wallflowers are still going, or coming, strong, and the bells of the lilies-of-the-valley, whose progress I have watched from the first stubby many-rooted shoots spreading rather like a creepy-crawly, are open and ringing a sweet perfume, just as good as I expected.

June

Flaming June – it is not only the fiery globe throwing heat across the empty heavens I think of but the great rash of poppies, opening full out so suddenly while the cooler late Chinese peonies stay clenched. Quiet Welsh poppies that have seeded themselves on the bed by my back door were out in May and continue if you dead-head them. Close to on warm days they smell of boiled sweets, peardrops. The Icelandic poppies, oranges and lemons, larger versions of the Welsh and red-orange wild corn poppy, succeed them in June, along with the great gawdy floppy-petalled black-eyed pale orange, pink and red hairy-stemmed oriental poppies, beloved of painters such as Georgia O'Keefe. The headier, heavier scents come in the hotter months. The Shirley poppies, the cultivated form of the field poppy, will come later still in August.

Wherever they are not in the way of anything else, I let the orange-red corn poppy seed and from my window the dots of colour among the tangle round my compost heap at the bottom of the garden make me think of butterflies as they flicker among grasses. If you pick off the seed heads while still green and sappy, there will be a gout of rich yolky liquid. It has an insidious and strange smell, invigorating rather than sleep-inducing, astringent rather than sweet, with an after-flavour of nut about it – perhaps of iodine, and reminding me of the smell on our stained fingers when we took off the furry cases from the walnuts that used to drop over our fence from next door's wood long ago in Buckinghamshire. But I think it is next month's poppy, stunned, like us, in a normal July's heat, that brings back Tennyson's lines from 'The Lotus Eaters' to me. He knew all about weariness, hot or cold:

> And through the moss the ivies creep
> And in the stream the long-leaved flowers weep
> And from the craggy ledge the poppy hangs in sleep.

Maybe gardening is addictive more than metaphorically in that if we sniff as we weed and tidy, we drug ourselves. Certainly, there is no decrease in the popularity of herbalists.

Even when there is no great fire-thrower in the sky, there are poppies nonetheless.

The various pleasures of this month step down before one that is paramount, for June is the month for roses. However much one tries to keep a sense of proportion, the rose takes the centre. It is not fair to compare it with other flowers, for really it is not a flower – it is a symbol, an emblem. It is one of the kingpins of the imaginative life. Its relation to the outdoor world is as an element, as a primary is to colour, as a prime is in the world of number. A rose is to flowers as an apple is to fruit (the word that got translated into 'apple' in the description of the Garden of Eden originally referred more generally to 'fruit'. The strength of the King James' version lay in making it a real English apple for weak lusting English humans to slaver at the mouth over, not just 'pomum'.)

Moving from the Garden of Eden to my back door, very particularly my 'Golden Showers' has smelt beautiful in a cool June in spite of blackspot which has depleted the foliage. The first bud opened last month. The flowers do not last long and if I cut one as it opens, I put it in a flat modern Bristol glass bowl I was given for my twenty-first birthday by an aunt. It is really an ash tray and shaped like a squat round pouffe and the opening holds one open bloom nicely. Instead of the air in the room being embittered and choked with the stench of stale cigarette ash, it is perfumed by my rose. I don't have many flowers in the house. I prefer them in the garden; but rose is the one I do. For one thing, cutting them helps the bush.

Sometimes stronger than the smell of roses as the buds open is the smell of spray against greenfly. It is difficult to know how long to risk waiting for ladybirds to do the job for you. Perhaps one thorough spray when the new leaves are opening and before the ladybirds hatch would deal with aphids that winter-over so successfully in our recent mild winters, without killing off the gardener's great ally. Soap suds also sometimes have the desired effect, but by mid-June in a good year the ladybirds should have taken over if not killed by spray.

During a few days in London at the beginning of June, 'It was roses, roses all the way/And myrtle mixed in my path like mad' kept coming into my head. Everywhere red and white and yellow roses were exuberating. I have never been anywhere in England where roses did not grow, almost better in scruffy backyards or by factory sheds than in the grand gardens where there is so much else of quality, and yet they retain their uncommonness.

We think of the rose as typical of English gardens, cladding grey stone walls in villages in green England, but it is native to the Middle East. There is a story of an eccentric (English) woman who had a fabled garden somewhere near Petra (that 'rose-red city half as old as time'). Travellers received a welcome there and it was said that she grew more than roses. Poppies and roses after all flourish in the same conditions. However many roses you see, and if you have bent a thousand times, or a thousand times twirled a cut rose before your face, the wonder of their surprise and the astonishment of their scent is never diminished. There are so many different sorts and smells. Some even that do not smell – although I don't see the point of growing a rose without scent; the ones that smell are not less glorious to look at.

My floribunda, a light crimson which I see through my back door when I sit at my kitchen table, refreshes my nose as it lightens my eyes. Its smell is fresh but not very sweet, on the side of crisp cut green leaves of cabbage, slightly astringent, like clean stiff table napkins. Round the corner, my creamy 'Peace' rose has the heavier sweeter perfume one expects of the grander larger roses which one prunes hard in March to get the stronger single blooms. The floribunda, which has the longest season, I do not exactly prune but just cut off anything dead, or weak and wambly, whenever I see it, and cut the dead flowers off before they go to seed. Also, being near the back door, it gets nearly as much tea as I do and is probably less damaged internally by this addiction of mine than I am.

There is a rose which perfumes the room, no, the house, it is put in, let alone the air round the bush, but which I don't really like the look of as it seems the wrong colour for a rose – magenta, like some car upholstery. This is *R. rugosa*. As my neighbour, giving me one, perceived, its really gorgeous scent has a hint of sweet not stringent lemon about it. I put it on my kitchen window-sill and each time I came into the house I felt that something exciting was going on – almost like coming into a house and hearing someone playing the piano in an upstairs room. There is such activity in scent going out on the airwaves. The smell is not at all magenta in tone. I shall plant one next winter, perhaps down among my rough 'meadow' grass, a white one if I can get it. It is hardy against insects, having a tough grooved dark green leaf not like the thinner ordinary rose leaf. I think they like to be in full sun though, and each year the shade of the beech trees over the road at the bottom encroaches further up my garden.

I got a quite different smell, though still of rose, when on a hot sunny day early in the month I called on someone who lives on the steep side of a hill looking south. At the bottom of the path leading to their house, on a bank above the road, was a sweet briar all in bloom, delicate fragrance in sun after shower, like the light spring fragrances. If I had to have only one rose scent, perhaps it would be you, good humoured little unpompous sweet-eye.

No, I could not choose. Whichever rose I am inhaling 'now', that is the one. There is 'Albertine', pale pink but not so pale as to be indefinite, profuse, now covering the railings on the other side of the road my front door gives on to. I can look at it from my table by the window in my front room, and every time I go round that corner, a fresh and beneficent waft reaches me above the smell of car exhaust from the road. Sometimes from my upper room I notice people who are out early, either walking dogs or walking off bad dreams or insomnia, or just in the habit of having the very best of the day to themselves, and they stop and smell the blooms hanging over the pavement, but seem too shy to do so later with more people about. Then there is the 'Bobbie James' that has been made to festoon with stars a neighbour's old apple tree, giving it a second flowering of a sweetness more like philadelphus than apple. Then there is . . . But there are so many and, as I said, roses are a little apart, so I have mentioned some more in a list at the back of the book.

The lupins, out in May, have given perhaps the greatest value all through June. Weeding by my path, head down on a sultry afternoon, I got a spicy but soothing smell as if someone's health-giving presence was alleviating the effect on my neck, shoulders and nails of grubbing about among broken concrete. I straightened up and there was my neighbour's pink lupin. It is pepper-spice without the harshness to the nose of kitchen pepper, and my own patch of lupins, on the edge of my raspberry bed (and intermingling, bringing the bees to the raspberries or vice versa as raspberries flower earlier and fruit when lupins flower) answers the fatter sunnier lupin across the fence. It is one of the best smells, very free on the air, long-lasting, refreshing – and haunting. Lupins, and the popping of lupin seeds in the heat of childhood summers, the too many grey furry pods of lupin in overwhelming flat heat of tired late afternoon on a bare flat lawn when one is five, furnish the garden of my mind. That also was limestone country. Lupins do well in thin soil, seed themselves, divide easily, and yet look and smell so cultivated.

Even when June seems a drab month, with no sequence of days when you leave the windows wide all night and don't even notice you've left them open (the air at midnight as calm and balmy as at midday), many scent-laden flowers open. The day lily doesn't mind cold in June as much as we do. I have some clumps of a sweet butter-yellow lily that has been giving out scent all month and at the end of June is still heady on the air. Near one clump and opening after it there are glowing violet dainty Dutch iris but their scent, as is the shape and the light way the head poises on the stem, is delicate, so that I can't really get it as the day lily over-rides it. Iris need hot sun to bring out their perfume.

As well as the lily there is another basic, as essential in its turn as the wallflower but of shorter duration – the sweet william. That is out in full scent this month while a few blooms of wallflower – that extraordinary, almost round-the-year flower – still add perfume to the air. Dianthus is a large family, each member delightful and fragrant in its way, but the sweet william is my favourite. Its whiskery buds reassure us of future pleasure as the end of May turns into June, while the later carnation's leaves are thickening into fleshy spears of beautiful grey-green. Sweet william's clovey smell is without the bitterness or sickliness at the back of the strong clove. Carnations, although sometimes lovely, remind me, when smelt close to, of a glue we used as children that turned my stomach. They are out next month but in June, as well as enjoying my sweet williams which do seed and spread themselves with a little help, I am ensuring a smell-bank by sowing seed of wallflower and sweet william. Planted out in autumn they will winter over with any luck and be ready to make May and June next year pleasurable.

Although we think of June, midsummer, as the apogee to which flowers open, like almost every other month it is sowing time for some, and for others the time to plant out seedlings with a view to next year. Thus, while I am relishing the gratifying fact that my Brompton stocks, sown last July and carefully protected through the winter to give May one of its chief delights, seem to be going on and on this year, I am planting out the annual Ten Week stock I sowed in the spring. Gardeners do indeed look before and after, at the same time living, as no one else, in the now of the nose.

A clump of astrantia is succeeding to the smell from the purple flower of the honesty that (now drabbing with seed pods in one of its transformations) scented my path leading to my back door whenever I went out there at night in May. In the sun during the day, the honesty flower sometimes gave off a sickly smell like flour paste. I have clumps of astrantia at the foot of a rambler that goes over the eastern wall of my garden and is out next month. The astrantia and the rambler are prolific and spread rather rampantly giving good value. Because the astrantia glimmers in the dark with its silvery-white slightly shiny flowers (the upstanding stamens within the star when the flower is open give it an off-white greenish tinge), I put some where nothing much grows in the poor soil under the yew by my back door and it flourished there as in the open. In May it just smelt papery but now that it has opened the bees are at it during the day. Sometimes it smells a bit like a dog pelt, faintly sickening (perhaps when it is going over) but sometimes so sweet, and its sweetness is free on the air and honeys it when it is warm, and lingers after dark.

Pansies, of course, go on, and my calendulas, as fresh as lettuce, are flowering. I have a patch of the orange ones which, especially at dusk, glow like a very strong lamp by my broad beans, which are podding and whose flowers continue. Some years it is hot enough for wafts of heavy scent from them to travel across the garden. The leaves and stem of the calendula also give off its individual scent all through their growing season, which can be most of the year. It is strong not rank, although perhaps an acquired taste. Its pungency is one I like and it pleased and refreshed me as I dug a whole lot of seedlings out of my vegetable patch, leaving some to keep the blackfly, so they say, off the beans, but really because that orange is so beautiful next to the greyish-green leaf and polka-dotted white flower, and the smell suits the bean smell. I transplanted the calendulas to a rough stony part of the garden. They seem to grow anywhere up here, through cracks in concrete as well as in well-manured soil, but not, I think, in shade.

My nasturtium seed in the stony soil by the fence at the bottom has germinated and if the plants climb over it, as they are intended to, not only shall I have a curtain of strong green interesting leaves and bright flowers over my grey palings, but pungent leaves for salad as well. Of the calendula, though, it is the petals you can use in soups and salads not the stronger leaf. In that corner against my bottom wall, my philadelphus is in bud, the white very visible though the flower has not broken out yet. I am eagerly awaiting their opening as this is its first year and I have thought about it for a long while. I need something by my gate, since my lilac, over against it on the other side, is over now, of course, and looks poorly. I must cut out any dead branches and pull out the new shoots at its base. I think of lilac and laburnum as linked, and both connected with storms, but laburnum succeeds to lilac and the purple lilac and the louring thunder clouds we occasionally get in May go together; a biliousness is sometimes brought out of the yellow of the laburnum by the ominous air of a June storm.

Now that the tulips that stood me in such good stead all May this year have died down, I will get their bulbs out. Daffodils, grape hyacinths, most bulbs, I leave in but tulips, very prone to being eaten and to rotting, I (in principle if not always in practice) take out. This year, I mean to store the different sorts separately so that when I replant in autumn I will know where will be yellow, where red, where small, where grand. Of course I meant to do that last year, but . . .

I have planted out my seedlings of Ten Week stock which haven't grown much but haven't been totally demolished by slugs, snails, insects. And, great joy, a peony that I planted last year and which I had bought to be red and out in May, has opened into a pale pink fragrant June-flowering one. It was intended to be seen from my loft window, a splash of dark red at the end of the garden beyond the apple tree against the east wall. I shall not move it (they don't like being moved and it is healthy at the moment with frilly soft layers and cool delicate lovely scent to match) and although invisible from up here in the house, unless you know it's there, it provides the most lovely fragrant stopping point when I'm pottering about on the grass by my apple tree.

I hope it adds its scent to the savour that passers-by on the road below might get from my garden – of citrus fruit peel and compost rot, sweet juice of the cut clover leaf (and, latterly, the honey of clover flower) and the whiff from the day lily still open nearby, together with the strawberries ripening and mouldering in the damp.

On the banks and in the hedges, the overbearing elder's yellowy-white lacy blossom is rather headachy too. Strange that such a rank-smelling tree, the smell of whose leaves and bark make me feel sick as a closed-in musty cupboard does, should produce such a fresh-tasting wine. I was once given a bottle of elderflower wine that was more deli-cate than a true Rhein wine. I felt I had taken a drink of a meadow in spring. Almost better – no, comparisons are odious not odorous – is a cordial, so simple to make that I have actually done so. You have to gather the flowerheads when they are open in the hot midday sun. The elder tree, like the hawthorn, attracts legends – gloomy ones at that. Perhaps things with strong smells stamp their personalities on that instinctive part of the brain where the sense of smell has its seat of operations.

I do not really like the elder, although if I could look at it as if it were something else, I would acknowledge it is a fine tree that gives good value far and near; if I could think of it as a rowan for instance, which I do like but whose scent, strong in May and now turning to berries, some find offensive.

Black clouds are gathering. June, which is ending, has been oppres-sive. It has all been a bit overwhelming. Though the over-riding smell of a sunlit end of June is a mixture of philadelphus and strawberries, if it gets too hot there is an arid dusty smell, the smell of rank stinging net-tles (although the dead nettle has a sweet smell). If we get rain after dry heat at this time, an almost delirious richness comes from all the wet foliage. I was in a doorway of a launderette one such June evening and someone came through from the back to look out at the street and up at the sky. 'I thought I smelt rain,' she said, and both of us stood and drew in the change in the smell of the air as the rain came down.

It was a terrific storm that night: a huge elemental drama, noisy and spectacular, to mark the turning of the year away from the solstice. Next day, apart from the refreshment and relief at not having to water baked earth and gasping plants, the storm could have been an illusion of a feverish night, so calm and clear was the early morning.

It was obviously going to be a hot day. I went out early down through the garden where the light was making the air round every blade of grass, every little drop of moisture, dance with its sparkling. The birds were having a lull after their earlier activity and it was quiet, but the flowers, grasses and bushes on the verges and in the hedges I walked past, seemed alert to the opening day, drinking in the moisture and the strengthening light equally, at the fullness of their sappy growth.

Later in the heat I might seek protection of the wood, to be invigorated by the savours of trees and undergrowth and the mast from our beeches that keeps its moisture through the most blazing summers. For now, I wanted to be in the open and the light, before the sun became dangerous, a great fiery gong in the sky. I came back as it was beginning to make itself felt, sucking out the odours from all the wet growth in field and hedgerow.

As I hastened back through my garden, the gentle now warm waft of air brought me a mingling of allium, calendula, feverfew, strawberries (and wild strawberries which have a different tang). The philadelphus dominated at my back gate and up the path, then was joined by roses, poppy, honeysuckle and sweet pea. There was vetch, clover and grass, where I had scythed the bottom 'wild patch'. Perhaps my new Chinese pale pink peony was a whiff mixed in with this and maybe some wall-flower. There was rue and rosemary (but the rue planted away on its own as it is not a good neighbour to all plants).

I went into the house to have some breakfast, adding the smell of coffee and buttered toast with ginger marmalade to June's bouquet which was coming in through the open back door from all over the gardens and the roads and air beyond. The gong of the sun was struck. I was where I wanted to be for midsummer.

July

July should be the time when the beating sun pounds the aromas out of the leaves on the mortar of the dry earth. Sucking the juices out of the earth, the heat opens the blooms so they release their allurements to insects onto the air.

In England there are such times: when the unremitting scrape of grasshoppers goes with the tickly smell of dry hot grass, when the vibration of bees in lavender reminds one of times when one desperately sought the merest line of shade, creeping by dog-sour walls in back streets; when to cross a square or an open field in the blinding light was a risk compounded of rubbish-gorged flies and splitting headache. The odours associated with pleasure at such times were the ones connected with the coolness of dim clean rooms, freshly-washed tiles, cold water running in a basin to wash off dust-encrusted sweat, insects and bits of chaff, the revivifying astringent smell of salad in a bowl, lemon drinks, cold fruit fools, junket in a cut-glass bowl with nutmeg grated on top, a jam jar of cut mint like a bouquet on the kitchen table, roses exuding from a polished table in the hall, bowls of sweet peas to bury the hot face in; or of going into a wood where the general odour from years of leaf fall, unrummaged, undesiccated by the sun's remorseless shafts, gives reassurance of moisture. The fresh impetus in the twenty-four hours that comes as the shadows lengthen and the sun cools its breath towards evening, quickens the tempo again after the afternoon slump and we come to once more at the dawn of night, so to speak, and the re-invigoration of the senses.

The olfactory pleasures of great heat are largely those that come at the cooling, the dampening of dusk, or the freshness that a shower or soaking thunderstorm brings out of the earth when it is heating up again and, of course, at night. As the earth cools or steams up into a sparkling early morning, the evaporating moisture brings the smells into the air, and there are flowers which open at dusk or in the dark to attract the moths and other nightflyers.

The smell of heat itself for me, the smell of heat in summer rather than the smell of summer, is the awareness by my senses of dryness, of warm dry stone, a lack of the stain of sap, of hot clean straw. Really, except for stones that have been in seawater and smell of it, the actual smell of stone is rather an awareness of the lack of damp, of no-smell. Stone being incorruptible does not rot, is not broken down as that word corruption implies, as vegetable matter is, and so does not smell except when the wet in it is breaking down some other matter. Well, that's my current theory. We are almost back to composting. You could try it out but although you're allowed to gaze at marble statuary and stand in the street and look at buildings (though you will be looked at if you stand and stare too long), if you went up close and smelt the different substances, you would probably be asked to move on.

For many, the height of summer is less comfortable than other times not only because heat dries us out together with the plants; our skin, let alone other parts, needs moisture – although not to the extent we have it some summers. Because these people suffer from conditions like hay fever, sinus infection or other respiratory ailments affecting the regions of the olfactory tract, their sense of smell is diminished and with this the batter on the senses becomes a source of misery instead of pleasure. With the route to the brain prevented from bringing in pleasurably all the rich goods that are usually incessantly being delivered, one begins to feel cut off, entombed in a bone chamber; one cannot think, as a sieged town cannot function for lack of supplies.

July begins the second half of the calendar and although it is the beginning of the end – only the night can lengthen now – it renews our images of summer, summer that should be day after day in which one can leave everything out to dry to the core, paint-burning days with the good heat drying out swollen timbers, drawing off the aches in our bones. Doors and windows are left open at night for days with no difference between the night in the room and the night outside, and going to visit someone needs no more than a sunhat and a toothbrush to carry. How simple and sociable life can be when you don't have to spend some part of every hour in activities resulting from perpetual change of temperature and atmosphere. How much time there seems. But, of course, through those open windows and into the lamplit rooms come the moths, and the biting insects; there is a particular horse-fly that lurks in long grass in July which can be really dangerous. And the July sun can be a dangerous animal, too.

I recall one occasion at the beginning of the month when I sat on my bench, so hot I needed to rig up the fishing umbrella I use as a shade. Nobody's motor mower was sawing the air into fragments and if there were a passing aeroplane drowning out thought, at least it passed. From my left came the scent of my roses, from my right waves of heavy sweetness from my neighbour's philadelphus in full sun, and they met just about where I sat. It was ten in the morning.

In the following days, whenever the fine weather made me absent-minded enough to forget my decision not to be lured into having a go at the plantains and clover and other bitter herbs so that my patch would be a grass one, the mock orange would flow over the acrid smell on my fingers (shepherd's purse was the strongest smelling of the weeds). There was still a whiff or two of a late lupin to go with it, sweet williams, too. These are worth dead-heading to lengthen the life of the plant. They are succeeded towards the end of the month by that later very strong clove-smelling dianthus, the carnation. I have a spray or two that grabs me over the edge of my waist-high bed by my back door and, especially after rain, I realize with gratitude why it is such a florist's favourite, but if I couldn't have both I'd have sweet william.

As I straightened up from my futile weed-grubbing, cursing my lack of discipline that had lost me the precious hours of lingering light evening, there was the philadelphus gleaming white through the hedge, throwing its sweetness. My own philadelphus, planted to shed perfume over the wall by my gate on to passers-by beneath, comes into its fullness a little later, being in the shade. It has a more elusive, more subtle orange smell not quite so profligate as the 'Belle Etoile'. I think mine might be *Philadelphus microphyllus*, described as a 'dwarf twiggy bush' and according to that book, apart from the fact that it is 'easy with masses of white flowers famous for far-carrying scent' it is a 'dull bush'. I can think of no more inappropriate word for it than 'dull'.

The flowers that make July the night-balmy time that, for me, is a

basic component of 'summer' are the white ones. Of the tobacco plants
and phlox at the end of the month, the white are the best. What glimmers still in my dusk are the silvery tessellated-centred stars of astrantia, sweet after rain, and everywhere the soft and almost hypnotic lamps
of oenothera, the evening primrose. They do smell during the day, but
on hot days by mid-morning they shut and look shrivelled and
finished-with. 'Must tidy those flowers that are over when I can get
round to it,' you think. Don't. By evening, they are new and fresh and
open; not crisp but gentle silk full of life with a delicate sweetness everywhere in the air to match their pale primrose-yellow. You can tell that
the sun is setting a little earlier now for the point at which the petals of
the blooms on the tall spike open into a cup, sometimes with a little
click of the 'ears' that support them, is moving back. For the lamps of
the oenothera in our open back gardens up here in the third week of
July, lighting-up time was 9.15.

But we haven't yet come to the best part of a summer night. Imagine
you are walking up to a house at ten o'clock one evening at the end of
July, rather warm and damp with summer rain. Perhaps there are some
shrubs at the gate, philadelphus gleams at you and dizzies you with its
sweetness. You reach the borders, two deep curves on either hand
beyond a wide strip of close grass edging the path, grass cut earlier in
the day and smelling now it is moist.

The path you are on is light, for it is pale gravel. The rest is dark, the
house with its alluring lighted window that throws an oblong obliquely
on to the gravel and makes the grass look artifically grey, is yet hidden
from you by a hedge (of box, perhaps) and a curve. To your right, you
suddenly feel a presence at shoulder height. People are watching you on
your private night wandering. You turn to face them and, as you do, the
spiciest and most delicious smell comes your way – not unlike lupin but
cooler somehow. It is the shoulder-high clumps of white phlox swaying

a little, glimmering and exuding a spicy perfume like a murmur. Here at last is the smell of slippery elm of my childhood, not after all from the pale June peony whose sweetness is more like rose and lily, nor the earlier lupin. At ground level at the edge of the border, the lighter-coloured pansies, yellow and white and pale mauve, are winking but they need hot day to bring out their fragrance to the full. There is the heavy scent of stocks and strong but sweet waft of tobacco flowers. There is mignonette.

Then you come to the house, and, rounding a brick wall, get a beautiful fresh scent of roses, almost of fresh-washed cotton in the sun with sweetness added, a daytime smell. Again, the flower is a pale one, not the heavily-scented red hybrid tea 'Ena Harkness' that gives out in the hot sun, but the climber 'Golden Showers', freshened by the night moisture after the heat of the day has sucked the colour from its petals from yellow to almost white.

Light is pouring from a window low on the ground floor. You can see in and it is like a stage-set, expectant, waiting for an entry. You are glad it is empty of people for you do not want to encounter eyes, or be asked in to start your part. A small table lamp is enough to make the whole house look solid with the contrast, a lamp that the moths, erring souls, have forsaken the beneficial lamps of evening primrose for, and all the pale flowers opening and giving off scent specifically for them. The lamp has no pollen, its attraction for the insects results in nothing but death. Why do the insects not take more notice of the calls of the sense of smell than of the fatal summons of the light? A wistaria, looking very black where the light catches bits of it, twists round the coping of the front door and above the window frame. In order to have an even stronger scent, let us have the rare white wistaria though the lavender one is pale and lovely enough. There is another sweet scent very free on the air, apparently coming from the window. Does the lamp-light, so soft and calming, after all carry a scent like a candle, and is that why it is lethal to the insects? Going to the side of the window, out of the shaft of the light, you sense rather than see, you certainly smell, copious but light like a wine that goes with fruit, the inconspicuous white stars of summer jasmine.

Above you a window, unlighted, is open. You imagine you are there. You have sat on, not wishing to break the last of the light by switching on the electric thus throwing the garden into premature darkness. The garden became more indistinct, then the sky dimmer and now it is the dark you do not wish to disturb. And you have your reward, for the night flowers have taken over the garden, and the night visitors. We could have a moon but we will not, for the most central part of this aliveness of the night, the most taking component, is a flower that you might not see even when it is open, for it looks like an untidy little bitsy of a weed. It is the night-scented stock.

We will come down to earth and give the stock its proper due later. This, of course, is not my house and garden, this garden where they have planted stocks beneath the windows (earlier in the year there were wallflowers there), where they have set honeysuckles to succeed each other, clambering over balustrades and arches, and formed pillars of roses to surround the stroller with sweetness through most of the seasons. Clumps of phlox succeed delphiniums and lupins at just the right height. There is alyssum in all the crevices on the terrace with lavender in troughs round it and a chamomile turf to cross to the house's french windows. It has a nice clean gravel drive to crunch along, this house, or a more obscure quieter path through the shrubbery at the back.

We will now return to my own unideal home where there are also those smells, apart from the wistaria. There is too little space on my frontage (or my backs) for a wistaria. There is only just room for a window. The one in the bathroom is low enough to smell the drifts of night-scented stock straggling over the bed by the back door, and from where I scattered seed in patches further up the side of the path in May. You get the best scent from them when you are not just by them, but when you have gone past, thinking you must do something to that dim and dreary and messy corner by the hedge. Then you get this heavenly surprise you have not been expectantly nosing for and realize you have done something about the corner – you have sown night-scented stock in May downwind from it.

As we come into it from the garden, the smell that greets us from the kitchen for most of a cold and wet, cold or wet, warm and wet, or hot and dry July, is soft fruit.

July is the first of the real jamming months, if you discount rhubarb and ginger. There is hardly a time, winter or summer, when the black-currant bush does not give off its healthy pungency, bark when there are no leaves, leaves as soon as they unfurl. The actual taste of the black-currants I like only in jam and purées and if I had to have only one jam I suppose this would have to be it. The redcurrant ripens a little later and the leaves, crumpled up, do not prognosticate the smell of the fruit as the blackcurrant's does. The redcurrant leaf smells just of hard green so the delicate sharp zizz of the most jewel-pretty of the currants is the more unique. If you haven't enough redcurrants to make redcurrant jelly, you can mix them with the first raspberries. Raspberries raw, stew-ing, jamming, pulping, take over my house during July, overlaying the richer, more irony smell of the blackcurrant – a contralto to a soprano.

But the early days of July are still an obsession with strawberries. In a wet July, you really do have your nose down among them for it is then a question of waiting for the readying fruit to dry off before you pick them but not waiting that half-hour too long and find oneself caught by the next curtain of rain putting paid to more of the fruit. Such a July can, in retrospect, seem a mixture of rotting fruit, fingers itchy with picking over bowls of sodden slug-attacked fruit only to find that one's hours of scrupulosity were wasted as all they were fit for was to add to the sweet smell of *compote de fruits* rising from the compost bucket in the yard. Add to this the smell of dank mouldering grass and sodden bonfire material, and perhaps the acrid billows of smoke of a bonfire, started wet if you have given up hope of any drying days.

There are two other quite different smells that linger through the damps of memory: the reassuring smell of handling leek seedlings which I never seem to transplant early enough to have fat leeks by November, and the pervading sweet smell of my privet flower when it is hot. I am always surprised when the flower turns out not to have the nauseous smell of some privet leaves. I think it may have been the smell of the leaves and stems in childhood that for so long linked this bush for me to stale neglected houses and dreary dark fronts, gloomy establishments in tiring roads to be avoided. A holly bush or hedge can be the same – it can be a splendid and interesting shelter or it can be the epitome of gloom and drear places. So, getting this strong sweet scent on the air and wishing to trace it I approach the privet flower gingerly, perhaps because its cream laciness reminds me of elderflower which can be overpowering. But my privet this year was nothing but sweetness.

I will leave cutting the hedge until after the flowers have turned into the large glossy black berries. I like it when I've clipped the hedge – a clipped hedge and mown lawn give you several pleasures, especially if you have let them get straggly; you can see more and you feel less scratchy and closed in on sullen days. It is a tiring job behind you that will last a little while, and your effort shows, like a line of clean washing flapping in the sun; you are doing the hedge or grass good even if you are jarring your shoulder and you are inhaling the pungency of cut green leaves and stalks – privet or box and, next month, yew and beech.

What is there to contemplate, all sweaty and dusty and fly-blown and scratched as I am, to reward me after this hedge-cutting achievement towards the end of hot hot July or in August before the coolth of the evening brings out the night smells, before the note of summer slides almost imperceptibly towards the different key of another season?

There is alyssum, free on the air in all this heat now, there is Ten-Week stock flowering and still, incredibly, my Brompton stocks that perfumed May; and there are sweet peas.

For some years now, sweet pea fanciers seem to have concentrated on producing blooms of tropical size and interesting colour combinations, and even the varieties that say 'fragrant' on the packet have not seemed to produce that fresh uncloying sweetness that my memory of a bunch of sweet peas expects. I think the other flower in the same class of delight for me would be the lily-of-the-valley. I was beginning to think that maybe it was my memory that was at fault. Perhaps I had got to the stage when spring wasn't like spring any more, when summers weren't hot, and when nothing smelt or tasted or felt quite so essentially what it was when I first encountered it and formed a pattern in my brain. As I was coming to terms with this possibility, we had a gorgeous spring, I do not remember such a summer *and* I grew some sweet peas that smelt as they used to. Indeed, they are called 'old fashioned' and are like small butterflies of clear colour (large for small butterflies, small for sweet peas nowadays) and every two or three days all through July and August the house has been refreshened with little pots and odd jars of sweet peas here and there on shelves, by stairs or bookcases, by doors. Their smell fades after a day or two but, of course, the more you cut the more they come so in this case the more you give away the more you get.

There is a different, beany, smell from the bright pink perpetual wild pea straddling my fence at the bottom. At this time, you will also get a second flowering of broad beans if you cut them down when the first lot of beans finished last month. Other beans are flowering and podding now. I grow French beans as a sort of edging and, quite apart from the staple of the runner beans for meals in August and September, I would always grow one or two runners up a small wigwam for the flower and the plant's enthusiastic growing – Scarlet Runner is a properly flamboyant name for a gay and noticeable plant; it is so mobile and full of life.

Now on our plates at supper, everything except a lump of cheese is from garden or allotment, and has usually been in the ground not much more than an hour before we eat it: early potatoes (Arran Pilot this year – not always easy to get. My maincrop Desirées have been flowering for some time so, as I get the earthy smell from digging up potatoes, I'm getting a different smell from the plants flowering in the next rows), carrots, the strong turpentiny smell of whose leaves and root as you pull them attracts the carrot fly, so you have to be careful to remove all foliage and not leave any thinnings around. The smell of them cooking is much sweeter than when they are in the earth, and when you gently sink your teeth into a soft but not over-cooked young carrot you can understand why they used them in the war to make jam. Next to the orange carrots on your plate, you might add a few of the pale grey-green late broad beans, to me the best-smelling but not the most useful of all beans; and, smelling of nothing very much but a green succulence until you slice and cook them lightly in a greasing of butter and some garlic and herbs, the first courgettes. From the end of July there begins to be a general smell of onions; not because you're cooking but because you may be drying your shallots.

The feverfew flowers (once one of the large chrysanthemum family but now classified as tanacetum) are mainly going over now, succeeded by clumps of other daisy-type flowers. The leaves are bitterer than earlier in the year but there are new shootings, and always you get a strong and, to me, refreshing smell when you handle the stalks, even the dead brown ones you're cutting down. The smell I get from rue, from similarly brushing my hand through the plant's growth, is to me the height of this sort of refreshment. Its yellow flower is going to seed now. It is a useful plant in that it remains green and cool and sappy even in this time of drought and I fondle it and breathe its light curranty aroma whenever I pass it. Every part of the plant is aromatic and even the blue-green colour of the leaves are soothing to the eyes. Another plant whose every dead twig still carries the unique scent of its flower is lavender. Any time you brush past a bush, you release a strong scent into the air and you can feel the oil on your skin afterwards.

Now free on the air are the conventionally acceptable odours of carnation and roses. The leaves of the pelargoniums are less unpleasant than when enclosed in the kitchen during the winter. You will be getting this rather catty smell on your hands now if you are taking cuttings, July being the time generally suggested for soft-wood cuttings, but with pelargoniums and geraniums almost any time you have a healthy-looking shoot that hasn't flowered, it may well take. Added to my scarlet and my pink pelargoniums which I have put in their pots in the bottom of the dark yew hedge so it looks as if they grow out of it, I have put two recently acquired scented geraniums by the path: one has a little white flower and a stipple of scatty leaves and a light menthol aroma; the other, a thick furry darker leaf growing closer to a fleshier stem, smells stronger and very medicinal. Both are head-clearing and refreshing with an effect similar to a whiff of ammonia, but neither as lovely as the sweet light-leaved scented geranium whose perfume is used in Rose leaf geranium soap and powder.

Other plants whose aromatic strength we associate mainly with the leaves are also flowering towards the end of this month and into next: lemon balm, winter savory, dill, fennel, calendula, nasturtium and that variety of savoury and decorative nasturtium called canary creeper – *Tropaeolum peregrinum*.

The sweet william is over but the wild strawberries are continuing with the pansies. My hypericum bush whose golden flowers had a golden honey-scent is covered in berries and most of the privet flowers, that heady sweetness, are fruiting. The main target for the bees just now is one large sunflower, across my ash path from some big splashy dahlias (a target for earwigs, alas). One could almost say the smell drips from this sunflower. It seems honey already. The bees will also be at the lime trees. I have not one in or near my garden but the other day going to a garden party in true garden party weather I rounded a corner not thinking of trees, plants or the sensations from them, but of hair, hat, time, and state of stockings. I was stopped by almost a blast of sweet sticky scent. I thought there must be a late philadelphus or some exotic flowering shrub behind the palings I was passing, in grateful shade for it was a broiling day. I stopped, sniffed, looked around. I was under a lime tree. Several times that day I made sure to walk that way and each time was taken off my guard at the strength and the defined area of the scent.

August

I have to admit to a prejudice against August. It is so often a tired headachy stagnant month, cloudy and close with ratty winds and wet, or if not wet, dusty and stale. 'Fly August' I think of it as.

The apogée of growth has passed. You look at the heavy restless foliage of chestnuts, sycamore, even beech and ash, and think, 'There's no more growth in you this year. You're over. You stand there in a sort of sulleness. Summer has shot its bolt. What we haven't done now can't be caught up on. There are no more chances.' A great tree in spring and at the height of summer is like a city. Now its business is in abeyance, as in our human metropolis. The fresh green succulence of the first leaves, which by midsummer had imperceptibly become the solid infill of whispering shade, has darkened, and the leaves become harsh and lustreless and brittle.

Sometimes sitting in an enclosed garden at a time that you are meant to be enjoying as holiday time, when all the work of spring should be visible round you as achievement, weariness and disappointment have made the very trees seem tired. Maybe it is not just an imagined anthropomorphism – maybe the arrest in plant life does mean they are less a source of energy and refreshment for us. The very name August is the only one of the names of the months that has that long weary drawl in its vowel.

It is, perhaps, partly on account of August being, for a large part of most people's lives in England, loaded with anticipatory anxieties. All our investment of hope in a successful holiday is focussed on the same two weeks year after year, usually the same two weeks as other people's. If we have not chosen correctly, if the weather is not right for the holiday we've planned, if, when it comes, we are not in the mood or ready for the sort of place where friends had a wonderful time last year, if the child that gets tonsilitis does go down with it as you repack the sunhats and the bathers for the last night-before-we-leave time, if (a shameful secret we keep to ourselves) we would rather stay at home and go away another time, or not go away at all, if people who were well and entertaining and pleasant company when this treat was looked forward to are now unwell and miserable and with their minds elsewhere, we cannot use our good sense, we cannot do what suits the season and us in our season.

We have cooked our one and only goose, costly goose not only in terms of money. Our reputation for success at enjoyment is at stake, our credit in the memory bank is at stake, and we cannot, dare not, say 'I'm not hungry just now' as we struggle with the bird to the table. We can only shut our eyes and think of September.

Even if it is not programmed in our genes that September is a beginning (and I would not be surprised to learn that the pricking up of our ears again once August is well and truly behind us proved to be part of our animal nature), for many of us the start of school, and all that is arranged in relation to the academic year, has engrained in us the experience that the year begins then. That is when things happen, when the engine of the year starts up again. You have a chance to set off, try again, turn over the old leaf.

So August for me seems in some ways more the end of the year than the height of a season and for some time I have stayed firmly at home in that month. It is like January in that it is quite a good time to work as people are either in retreat or away with their own families – and not away visiting me, either.

Once you modify your ideas of what you're supposed to be doing in August, it can have many pleasant attributes, other attributes than thundery atmosphere, flies and tiredness. It is not always, or all the time, wet and disappointing or sultry and heavy and faded, and if you stay at home, when it pours with rain and the clouds lour and the trees toss in distress at approaching storm, you can get pleasure from the fact that you cannot today cut the grass that the rain is making grow luxuriant. Bless your lazy temperament that you are inside with a book and not trying to convince five children and three adults that you get the best view of the real Dartmoor plodding and slithering in driving rain with uninviting sandwiches banging against your thigh in your pocket and your eyes on your boots or the broken strap of some obstinate person's inadequate sandal.

Of course, in going on about this, I am taking my revenge for past malaise and failed expectations. Nothing apart from sheer tiredness makes one as bad tempered as hope cut off, and by August we are tired of the year. Another advantage of staying at home this month is that there's quite a lot you can be doing in preparation for next year. In fact, August includes, as compensation, some of the best smells.

August is a time of vegetables and smells of leaves and roots as we clear: dusty musty smell of old growth. What flowers you have in August depends on how diligent you've been at dead-heading earlier. I've got my second round of canterbury bells (I suppose we should not expect smell from them as well as their ringing beauty) and broad bean flowers. Dead-heading continues to be useful now, along with beginning to clear for autumn activities.

One early evening at the beginning of August, I came back from my allotment with potatoes, carrots, shallots, beans (broad and runners), kohl rabi, and a little tomato, and soon the juice of the runner beans under the knife mingled with the smell of other vegetables cooking. After supper, through the open back door, the pale cups of the oenothera and the sweet Turkish smell of the night-scented stock, the clovey smell of other stocks, and the deeper clove of carnation, took over. Then there was the fresh astringency of a perfect unfurling bud of 'Golden Showers', lemon balm up the path, and then phlox.

But what had drawn me into the darkening garden were the night-scented stocks, and it is the one smell that, inside, comes to me on its own without seeking it out. This is one of the high points of the year – the quiet house, the lamp on the table with the bowl of sweet peas, dahlias in a jar on the shelf. It is so still there's hardly the flap of a moth. It's warm enough again, after the dip we took at the end of July, to relax and think of another day's activities ahead in and out the house, pegging down strawberry runners, taking cuttings of honeysuckle, of pelargoniums, remembering not to miss the time for sowing spring cabbage; drying shallots and then onions in the sun, cutting down the broad beans for a second flowering, and being reminded, by the smell on your hands when you touch stalk and leaves, of excitement at the emergence of those grey-green leaves at the beginning of the year if you had done a sowing in the previous November.

August is a bridge: dead-heading, we remember a little sadly the surging season of growth passed. We are thinking of the autumn; soon we'll be preparing for the spring. You get all the scents as you dead-head, from plants still flowering as you stoop among them and the aromatic scents of stalks as you cut feverfew, calendula, lavender, lemon balm. Then, of course, indulging in a splurge of spending at the increasing number of shops that sell bulbs, and sorting out the bulbs that you may have lifted from your own garden earlier, you get, mingled with the smells of August, the imagined smells of tulip, hyacinth, narcissus, crocus. It is the whiff we get off hope. Doing something now for spring, just at the point when we may have little patches of dread about the end of summer, somehow diminishes winter, as if it will be simple to jump over it to the other side.

But to return to the smells of August, which, like its atmosphere sometimes, are the heavy ones. Maybe you will take a pause from work on a morning at home at the beginning of August (you cut the grass yesterday in the coolth of the evening after a thunder shower and you are sensibly not going to start painting the bathroom until the coolth of this evening). You sit on your bench which is on the brownish patch (you would not call it grass unless you were an estate agent) behind what is meant to be your rose-bed. Your bench, too, needs painting but, having omitted to do it in the spring, you decide there is going to be plenty of suitable weather for that in autumn. There is a smell of old paint flaking and wood baking. You remember not to rub your hand along the edge or you will get splinters. You get a long cool drink or, if you are really dry, hot tea, perhaps from the mint that you have prevented going to flower by picking it earlier, or mint you dried last year (I prefer mint tea from dried to that from fresh). It is too hot to bend and weed which is when one gets the most benefit from pansies and the low sweet flowers in the borders but now above the fragrance of the tea carried to you by its steam, easing to the sinuses, or the smell of cucumber and mint and fruit from a bedewed glass, you will receive free at your nose the scents that are plentiful on the air at this time.

Carnation has succeeded to sweet william. I am glad I have carnation in my garden to mingle its heavy clove with other smells and I love rounding the corner of my shed and being welcomed to my back door by the gush of scent from some that sway from the raised bed there. A bunch of separate carnations to stick in a vase is not, however, my favourite presentation, although goodness knows if anyone gives flowers of any sort it lifts the ego in a special way. There is the scent of roses coming from the corner and mignonette, which I appreciate as precious as an ingredient but don't personally like all that much on its own. There are stocks, which I am crazy about, and, competing for best smell of the month and very different, the subtler sweet-spiced phlox. There are the late very sweet small stars of the wild clematis, known as traveller's joy in flower and old man's beard when it is whiskery with seed at the end of the month. There are still some *Papaver somniferum* (opium poppy), open and floppy with the heat like people who have over-indulged and can't hold in their stomachs, and a dot here and there of the slighter clear field poppy, especially if you pulled off the seed heads while green, making the yolky pungent sap gout. In fact, if you prevent almost any plant going to seed, August need not be a time of going-over and tired tangle in the garden. At the end of the month, one of my canterbury bell plants, a dainty single white, was budding for a third innings, and my Brompton stocks seem to have turned into everlastings.

There is the ubiquitous calendula – shoot, buds, flowers, seed heads and new seedlings all strongly aromatic. My thyme has long since flowered but winter savory, lemon balm, marjoram, mint, all thought of mainly for their leaves, are flowering. There is some lavender.

You will probably have harvested your shallots and they will be spread out to dry. The foliage of some of your main onions will have withered to straw at which point they're ready to come up. I think I, as well as the house, must smell of onions in August for I spend my time when I've lifted them putting them out at any sign of hot sun to dry off, and at the threat of rain, or before I go out or to bed at night, bring them in, feeling, as with washing nearly dry in a wet season, that it is a pity to waste all one's efforts so far for lack of a few minutes spent moving them in. Both houses I've lived in since I've grown onions have had a bathroom with a flat unshaded roof and this is the best place to put them although it can involve climbing out to retrieve the onions several times a day and getting black in the process. There have been years when the family, coming back from holiday expecting hot water to get themselves and clothes clean, a welcoming meal and a tidy house for them to spread their effects over, have been greeted by a strong smell and warnings to watch where they put their feet – not onion soup to sooth and revive them or a new carpet but damp onions spread out on newspapers on the floors. This obsession with drying them properly pays off, for in a good year we've still had usable onions beyond the point where I'm sowing the new sets in March.

In August, though, for me phlox is pre-eminent, especially if you have insisted on white phlox. They are best towards the end of the day and, with the tobacco plants, come into their own in the dark. If you pick a floret when it is going over but before it is brown and leave it to shrivel indoors, you will have perfume from that all winter. The white nicotiana are also best, as with most fragrant flowers that come in different colours, although the dark red or maroon can smell good, too.

In fact, if it is warm, August nights are sometimes better than the days, which is a good thing as night is impinging more and more, another reason for feeling uneasy and discontent. By the end of August, it will be getting dark at eight in the south. The shadows spread further earlier (or, as my allotment neighbour, said to me, 'It's getting late too early'); the hedges move a step nearer, like grandmother's footsteps, while your back is turned. We are being pushed into a smaller space, the horizon is being reeled in.

At either end of the day, the light is less strong in its fight with the dark, but before this happens stroll in the garden late, or perhaps to get a little air if you can't sleep, sit on the bench that was too glaring at noon, and the presences of tall ghostly flowers will make themselves felt: clumps of phlox and the pale yellow lamps of the evening primrose that shine with a strange exciting light, and whose smell is delicate but plentiful. These flowers seed themselves everywhere and one year I decided only to have them where I wanted them – a stately accompaniment down the garden path and another row which would rise up and look over the privet hedge that makes a sheltered square of my upper garden. But, of course, I was not firm enough, and luckily the flowers knew better than I did how they would be most delightfully useful, and from the corner of what if I were a euphemistic (ie lying) estate agent I would term 'level lawns', from among the roses, from the midst of my raspberries and towering above them, from the fence, from gaps in the concrete of the path, singly or in clumps where they were not supposed to be, comes this ever surprising refreshment of the pale but clear open face of oenothera.

As you pass, they gently brush against you, there is nothing harsh about them, until the flowers give way to sharp scratchy long seed pods later in the month. They give solace and if you go out into the sparkling moist early mornings of late summer as a sort of aperitif to the day, as you may stand in the night-garden as a nightcap, they are still open and

71

fragrant. If the day is hot, you may think they are over, their blooms finished like wrinkled skins of burst balloons, but leave them – by evening, they will be as fresh as if they had just opened, revived by the oncome of dusk as we are by inhaling their fresh smell.

Nicotiana, the other night pleasure of late summer, of course does not see to itself as oenothera does and is among the tender plants one is wary about planting out too soon, especially if you live high as I do where the temperature can drop 20 degrees in the night after a hot day. But any trouble is worth it. They go on and on, especially if you plant them out in succession. They do smell during the day but at night, when you get their full impact, you realize that that had been only half-hearted in comparison with their night scent. If only those who smoke the leaves could smell half so nice as a result!

It is at night that I feel the truth behind *Alice Through the Looking-Glass*'s encounter with the flowers. At night, they seem to be waiting for you, as if someone has joined you without a sound. There they stand, not smoking in quiet relaxation, as I imagine the narrator in *Maud* who stands at the gate alone in the dark, but shimmering slightly, exuding fragrance and waiting for you and the moths to pass by. I think it is in this month when I am out in the garden in the dark that the fifth verse of Keats' 'Ode to a nightingale' comes so frequently into my head, although it is May he is referring to:

> I cannot see what flowers are at my feet,
> Nor what soft incense hangs upon the boughs,
> But, in embalmèd darkness, guess each sweet
> Wherewith the seasonable month endows
> The grass, the thicket and the fruit-tree wild.

As I stumble into the house, clumsy like some drunk bee, the honey of the alyssum outside my back door hits me, as does the cooler scent of the 'Golden Showers' rose, also free on the night air after a hot day. It is in August I get the full effect of my clumps of alyssum. I have exclaimed about this extraordinary plant in other months but if I am exact I would say that gratifying as it is from May onwards, when scrubby bits of straw-like plants that have survived from a previous mild winter are renewing themselves and new seed is germinating, one does not get the value one has come to expect of it until, suddenly one day, hot sun brings it out overwhelmingly. You check – almost like hearing the pips for the news and looking at your watch and yes, it is August. It was not, after all, that 'it's not quite so good this year' or that one's memory was better than one's nose, or that one is getting blunted in old age, but that we had not yet come to alyssum's olfactory peak. As I turn a corner at noon, the whole air is honeyed, the first warm August days bringing out its sweet accustomed scent. On hot days when the back door is open, it fills the kitchen. It goes on renewing itself for many months and in the day does what *Matthiola bicornis* does at night: reminds me that the most inconspicuous growth provides the major smells.

Apart from what you might sow in boxes indoors in March, the first alyssum to come up is the tiny pointed triangle from the self-sowing seed from last year's plants. By mid-June, when what you sowed direct into the ground in May, begins to be visible also, you will realize that with what has wintered-over, the self-sown plants and with what you have sown, you will not be short, but to my mind you cannot have too much. Although inconspicuous to the point of invisibility at first, and straggly and untidy when died down, when there is a mat of alyssum all out together, it gleams in the dusk and is quite something to look at. It is still fragrant in the dark although it likes the sun, whereas you have to wait for the night for *Matthiola bicornis*.

Ah, night-scented stock – little weedy spindly frizzle that if we forget where we have scattered the seed in May and are in one of those nervy tidying-up moods, we may well pull up as thin weeds – what is there to be said of you? You deserve not a paragraph to yourself but an encomium. You are the bull's-eye of this account, you are the omphalos of my song. Not all the perfumes of Arabia . . . but perhaps you were from Arabia before you became the essence of English summer nights at their ideal? (The gardening manual says 'from Greece' so the words 'Turkish confectionery' rising to my mind when I try, vainly, to describe your perfume may not be so wide of the mark.)

As with alyssum, rose, honeysuckle and jasmine, it can be an ingredient of a town summer night as well as a country garden one. These, the most expansive of perfumes, are in fact associated for me with summer in London. A honeysuckle (of which there is at least one that flowers in each season) will grow by the drabbest of basement railings in a little hole in the concrete; it is a woodland vine and is used to poor soil. However down-trodden your accommodation, your coming in and your going out through the months of alyssum, rose and honeysuckle would be by no means drab but luxurious. And if perhaps you haven't been able to occupy a damp dark basement even, and have no control over the area steps or the yard where the rubbish goes, but have to creep up through someone else's domain to a room at the top of the house, you could still put a pot or box of alyssum on a window ledge or, as some people hang a bird-cage, fix a container on the wall outside. Sit by the window open to a stuffy August in a town and smell that, and you feel the air has come to you across fields of flowers, as if the night were expanding and relaxing wherever that scent travels.

Well, we have got through the month with fewer doldrums than I expected. The rain was so needed around here that the dull days were a relief. They also served as a reminder that not for ever could one say 'tomorrow will do, leave it until tomorrow, it will still be dry and fair and hot tomorrow'.

Quite without planning it, I found myself starting to tidy up, cut down, making way for the next season, harvesting really. As well as marjoram, lovage, winter savory, thymes, comfrey, nasturtium, chive, mint, feverfew, rue, chamomile, scented geraniums, rosemary, sage, which remind you of their presence as you weed or pick things near them, the steam from the kitchen contains at this time an even greater variety of vegetable aromas than in July. I like growing beetroot, although don't want to eat much of it and prefer it as a hot vegetable than cold with vinegar. Its distinctive smell and colour contrast with bunches of crisp crinkly spinach, the stems of which, simmered and dipped in butter are as pleasant to bite into as asparagus heads, and such of the paler cabbage as the plague of caterpillars and other grubs have left, and the accumulating glut of runner beans and courgettes.

This is the time when, instead of a fruit bowl, I put a bowl of tomatoes on the table. Unlike plums (alas, for I love them) you seem to be able to be as greedy as you like with tomatoes without them upsetting your stomach. The plant is interesting and strong-smelling at every stage. It is the best fruit to take on expeditions being more thirst-quenching than a bottle of water over a longer period, and less sticky than oranges, but if put to ripen on a window-sill in strong sunlight will shrivel. They are much more comfortable in the dark of a brown paper bag with one ripe tomato for encouragement.

This year I tried to grow two plants whose refreshing savour I'd previously experienced only when bought from greengrocers – peppers, which I planted between the tomatoes so they got watered; and didn't I have to chose a year of drought to try to grow also the plant that has to be kept moist all the while, celery. The tops of celery simmering in the soup pot is, for redolence, the vegetable counterpart of phlox. My obsession with keeping moist my seed tray indoors in March, seedlings, transplanted seedlings, planted out seedlings, transplanted plants, seems to have borne fruit, or rather stalks and fresh green leaves.

A plant whose fruit when rubbed between the fingers has a sharp attractive healthy sort of aroma with echoes at the back of it is the hop. I have not yet tried adding it to my brew. I pulled up a root from a rubbish dump in a town one late autumn and stuck it by the prop that is holding up the rather unsightly cover to my coal bins here. And now the space between the tarpaulin and bin-top is all hung about with pretty green lantern-like fruits which, when crushed or rubbed (or stewed, I suppose), give off a smell of salty garlicky flavour. Also sometimes to be seen on rubbish dumps in strong green leaf just now, like tough dark spinach, is horseradish.

Why, you may ask, do I go on about smells that have to be coaxed out of stem or leaf by cooking, or minor, obscure smells from chance encounters in hedges, and ignore one of the major scented bushes in so many gardens, topping so many walls, free on the air, popular, honeyed: the buddleia, beloved of butterflies? The answer is, I don't know. I don't know why I don't like buddleia. I admit its smell can be lovely, enticing you, on a walk, until you come round the corner from which it's wafting and there is this dreary plant. I love lilac. Although not of the same family, they yet have not dissimilar shapes and colours. Is it the buddleia's dull leaves that put me off? Is it some memory, visually forgotten, osmically registered, of some low desolate cul-de-sac of an August afternoon, some ideal picnic spot sought that turned out to be a rubbish dump? I am trying to separate the smell from the association the plant has for me and learn to restrict my reaction to the threshold of the senses, but if I could do that I would also destroy the importance of smells. The insidious hold, the large life of smells, depends on this tangle of associations between the senses, in the same way as you can never restrict the impact of a word to its sound. A smell is hardly ever passive enough to be isolated. As the molecules permeate the air, so a smell will suffuse our experience of a thing. The French language seems to acknowledge something of this in that *sentir* used transitively is both to smell and to feel.

There is no question of my trying to reform my reaction to the major smell that starts at the end of August to dominate the house in autumn – apples.

I was sitting down at my desk on a rather dull day when this strong mouth-watering perfume filled the room. I had no flowers on my desk. I turned my head and remembered I had bought a big bag of Discovery apples and piled then up into a bowl on the window-sill, for their brightness as much as anything. The apples on my one tree – a Bramley – are swelled and the first one fallen. Soon I shall try it stewed with the blackberries I picked in fly-heat the other day, a sweaty day when the brambles and the nettles amongst gave off a wearying acrid smell. I don't like raw blackberries, so I am a good picker: none go in my mouth on the way to the basket. Nor do I like the cultivated ones for cooking. For the best jam and jelly, you need both apples and blackberries to be slightly on the under-ripe side – tart and shiny. Another interesting smell that lingers in the house for some time comes from the making of crab apple jelly. It has a faint clovey tang to it.

The elderberry with its irony smell has also succeeded to the fragrant flower. The bullaces, the sharp wild plums, are brightening some hedges with their orange-red where the traveller's joy has become the old man's beard, a soft curly silver beard when the flowers have just gone over into seed.

So August is the beginning of the gathering season as well as the harvesting of cultivated crops. There are lighter sweeter smells as well from two plants that will have a resurgence now if you picked sedulously earlier on – sweet peas and wild strawberries. Mingled with these are astringent smells of nasturtium, tomatoes, bonfires, new feverfew leaves, poppy stalks. How could anyone, how can I, think of August as a dull month?

September

On the clock of the seasons, high noon stands with its back to the winter nadir, pointing up into the blue lasting summer, but 9 and 3, the quarters, stretch one arm across to link spring and autumn, though on the other side they face away towards the extremities that come between them. If the calendar began the year with March, as it did at one time, then September would be midway through, high-water mark. That is so when using the tropical year as a measurement, for that goes from one spring equinox to the next. September is a sort of mirror-image of spring, back to back with March.

January may be New Year, and March, which is officially the beginning of spring, considered to be the beginning of the growing cycle, but the agricultural year starts in autumn and for me and many I know September has always been a beginning.

After harvest, when nothing can happen after the fulfillment of the cycle of growth but fall and rot; after the stasis, the stale, the finish of August, what follows is: beginning again. It is a circular twined chain that you can never quite unwrap to find a piece that is not linked into, dependent on, a before and after. It is said that a person's whole life flashes before them at death. September, the mirror of spring, can include attributes of all the seasons.

As much as March, it is seed time: harvesting and sowing. Some plants start flowering in autumn, but even when August has been (literally) a wash-out, making a first hot week of September seem like summer at last, our attention begins to be drawn more to leaves, stalks, roots, berries and seeds. Inevitably, we are moving towards preparing for the winter while we still have light and warmth, when clearing and cleaning, storing and putting away can be a pleasure, not an emergency to be done after the last minute.

In some years, the end of August becomes a fiery furnace and then September starts off smelling of hot dry fields, a sweet smell of dried grass and cut corn stalks mingling with bonfire smoke and baked earth; but dusk is beginning to creep in earlier, at first a hazing and dimming, then increasingly backing and spreading into the gently lit days, which at midday can make us feel that time has stopped and the calm clear ease will continue uninterrupted for hours and days.

With the dusk of such a day, the smell from the night-scented stock begins to flow into the balmy night air. The petals of oenothera, rags in the hot bright day, are crisping up their pale primrose-yellow lamps. The honeysuckle outside my back door wafts strongly with the more astringent, clean-linen smell of the 'Golden Showers' rose it is smothering. The smell of cloves from carnation and stock, and the honey of alyssum which took a new lease of life in August, had filled the day and the sweetness still lingers in the warm night.

At the beginning of a month, we still have the opportunity to do the things that belong to the season: that is, each month begins in hope. For September, it is harvesting and clearing what is there on the one hand, with a great deal of sharp acrid savoury smells from dead-heading, disentangling, weeding, cutting down leaf and stalk, digging up roots (including, of course, edible ones which one gets the smell from again when cooking). On the other hand, there are anticipatory draughts of olfactory pleasures to be had as one jumps six months ahead in one's imagination while planting bulbs. Since the imagination and the olfactory sense are inextricably meshed, one cannot say that the fragrant frail light scent of an opening daffodil dancing in a spring breeze mixing with the smell of leaf-mould and earth as one plants bulbs on a still September day is *entirely* illusory.

We still think we are going to live the season day by day, not just plan for when it comes, or catch up in retrospect. In the first three days of each month, I try and do a bit of as many as possible of the things I want to be doing through the month so it will be worth keeping them up, but there are too many. There is also too much of other sorts of business starting up again at this time, and this all comes with the sensual lulling, that illusion that the sun is staying in the sky for us, the earth is pausing in the year's turning to give us ease, opportunity, time. 'Indeed there will be time', and 'later' means more of the same, not a changed state.

A morning in early September: the sun is on the summer jasmine that grows through the end of a yew hedge like a tangled mane of hair. Long tendrils catch at me as, beckoned by the sunlit garden beyond, I go up the narrow path from my back door between hedge and hut. The savoury hop plant, growing up the side of the hut across the path from the jasmine, has joined it to make a sort of unstable arch. Each year the

81

hop grows over the hut roof, as I intend it to do, covering it with its green tendrils and wide leaves, and each year, just as it gets to the top of the slope, where it can be secured, we have a gale that sweeps it off. Now this heavy many-snaked vine is hanging in a sort of noose that would trap any tall intruder creeping down my path in the dark to my back door. (Mind you, no one except a cat could get down that quietly, there are so many old buckets, pots, cans, bits of wood, props, bits of guttering, to say nothing of two water butts, a rickety table and chair frames with loose seats, to trip over and set a-clanging and a-rolling. This untidiness is better security than those fierce lights that people nowadays illumine their back gardens with. They hurt one's eyes and prevent one seeing the moon and stars properly and enjoying the balmy dark of one's garden as the nights draw in while they are still warm, or indeed later in the year when it may be sharp and frosty on a glittering cold winter night. The wrong sort of light is as jangly and numbing of the senses as a blaring noise.)

It is going to be hot and an ideal day to get all sorts of things done, but it is also a good day to go down the hill to my nearest small town where there is a laundrette, an excellent hair-cutter, a variety of well-stocked charity shops; above all, there is still a good ironmonger. They have some autumn onion sets which I am thinking of trying this year. I also buy some ranunculus which can be planted in autumn or spring and this is a reminder to dig up the ones that flowered successfully earlier in the year.

I linger on the hill coming back, blackberries and sloes and hips and haws beginning to add what I think of as a hedgerow tang to the smell of the turf and the flowers in it and the dry chalky soil they thrive in. Under the trees that shade the steep stony track up the side of the hill, there are damper cooler smells of old leaf-mould and some of this year's fall drifting to the ground and beginning to join it.

At five o'clock on these days, there are still a couple of hours of light. Damp mouldering weather might return any day so I went down to the canal to pick some blackberries. They were rather going over. I find their over-ripe smell distasteful. That, mingled with some of the other smells by the canal, can be a bit sickening. There is an apprehension in the nose that, in among the dank weedy reed and duck smells that are not unpleasant to those who, like myself, find the paths and banks of any watercourse interesting, there may be something disgusting, some foul dead rotting thing corrupting the air. But, in fact, on this occasion, the canal didn't even smell particularly fishy or slimy. The cow parsley was dry and going to seed, the creamy white bells of the comfrey were still flowering. There was suddenly a moist fruit smell at a bend, mixed with the sort of chemical smell you used to get passing dry cleaners: bullaces had dropped their ripe fruit onto the path they shaded, and a bit further along there was a humming and vibrating coming through the brick wall of a factory building. When you walk along a canal even more than by a river, you are walking through the human history of an area, and your nose, as well as your other senses, will help alert you to this. There is hardly a season when canal or riverside is not an interesting place to be, but autumn is a particularly good time.

As much as I want to be in my patch every hour of the day and night, and not lose a minute of the fulsome dawdling, it is also often similarly nice in other people's places, and the September fullness and feeling of gathering activity after August makes it a time of year for visits.

There is a very particular area of England I like to be in at this time and that is Dorset, not far from the Hampshire border, on the heathland and the small bays at the back of Poole Harbour on the Isle of Purbeck. Here are the smells of the sea and the shore mingling with reedy river mouths, dykes and boats and meadows and pine trees. The more acid soil means that heather and bracken thrive. On hot afternoons in sheltered places, you can still hear the popping of the gorse flowers, exuding their coconut honey which mingles with the sharper sweetness of the heather and the dusty acrid smell of bracken on the turn to bronze and brown. There are all sorts of little low plants on heathland and on sandy headlands which release their astringency as you scrunch over them; there is a dominant smell very much of lemon. Sometimes there are bilberries ripening, and there is a resinous eucalyptus sort of scent that mingles with the smell of seaweed and mud when the tide is going out and the breeze is blowing off the waters of the harbour on to the land.

Mid one still September morning, I was sitting between oak tree roots lined with moss and dry gold-green-brown leaves, having walked down from a headland, through the sun-splashed woods of the plantation, down the farm track over open land to the shore. I was sitting under a tree but my feet were in the sand for here the trees come down to the shore, or the beach has come up to the woods. I was sitting in warmth and entire solitude and stillness looking across the water to the different-sized islands which are scattered on the expanse of Poole Harbour. There were one or two boats at anchor, tarpaulins over the cockpits. The last vestige of the weathered grey planks of a landing stage that I remembered, had long since disappeared. In the gardens of the inland villages I had come through, the flowers were luxuriant – fat-throated snapdragons, Michaelmas daisies, wonderful stocks and mounds of alyssum and nasturtiums on brick walls, but out here in the woods on the point and on the dunes and heath, the scents were of blackberries, sloes, bilberries; gorse and honeysuckle; pine, whin, sand and creosote; of oaks, their acorns beginning to drop and add a bitter nutty component to the leaf-mould, birches, seaweed and a tang of salt and wet iron mingling with the general woody smell of bracken, moss, fungi and rot.

Back home to catch up on my own patch I am digging up some potatoes, cutting bean stalks, getting rid of dead pea growth, leaving leguminous roots where possible to put back their nitrogen into the soil. Digging at mild dusk, I smelt a sweetish but sharp smell – surely that's not potato rot? No. Probably I'd touched feverfew plants near the potatoes which mixed with the dewy-damp potato fruits. Some of these had got squished into the soil I was turning and into the potato stalks as I shook them out and threw them on to the pile for bonfire. That is one plant I no longer put on my compost heap since there has been some incidence up here in recent years of blight and other potato and tomato disease.

During the day in the garden, there had been sweet peas (which, at this stage, I'm not picking for the house, as I want seed for next year), rather acrid dahlia, and stocks. These, I think, are the most generous with their sweetness of all the flowers. We must wait till night for the night-scented ones and then the oenothera will also come to life again. There are roses in the garden and, in the house, a crisp lettucy sort of smell from my cut orangey-red rose, so different from the heavy velvet sweetness of my dark red one.

There are smells from flowers which are not exactly flower scents – from the fleshy leaves and stems of the bright valerian growing in the wall, from the stale-cupboard smell of herb robert as I pull it out from between the stones. I am fond of herb robert; it was among the first wild flowers I learnt the names of when I was in north Devon as a child. I suppose its very personalized name linked it with figures in old stories like Childe Roland and Friar John. There are dahlias, calendulas, bean and pea pods, and the French sorrel leaves and stalks that squirt a piquant citronous liquid into your mouth and throat when you chew them, like those zizzy 'refreshers' you used to buy in little paper tubes, only more fruity and refreshing.

The flowers of the main crop of runners have mostly turned into beans by now, and the smell of them cooking pervades the kitchen. There is the fresh and green not quite cucumbery fragrance of courgettes picked small. There is the dusty astringent smell of nettles on hot dry days, apple peel and core in the sink.

Apples at different stages, from pecked or bruised windfalls in the wet grass, already smelling cidery, to the steaming apple pie coming out of the oven, pervade house, yard, shed and garden, and with various sorts of oniony smells, becomes the dominant smell of the season. Of course there is the smell of cut grass again and dandelion leaves and roots, for September is, second to March and April, the time for grass.

In spite of scent from some flowers still being free on the air, you have to go near to get the smell from what is still out, sniffing close up. Increasingly, it is the leaves and stalks, the earth, the hedgerows, the undergrowth and woods where we will recognize the odours of the season. Grass being cut two gardens away still brings an immediate pungency, juicy, fresh, recognizable, overlaying even the smell of traffic on the roads. While driving, I have suddenly smelt that a roadside bank has been cut and, lowering the window to let in the air warmed by mid-September afternoon sun emerging after rain, in spite of the petrol and diesel fumes and grit from the road I know will fill my nose, I have breathed in the soothing refreshment of wafts of cut grass instead and this has reassured me that I am not going completely anosmic after all.

We must expect dampening and earlier dark now. Go down the path on a wet mid-September evening: some oenothera are still out here and there, especially if you have taken off the main seed spike so the side shoots flower, but the scent is much more indeterminate. The double and Ten-Week stocks exude their smell of clove, the clumps of alyssum gleam through the dark. They do smell even at night but for their best effect need high noon heat. Tobacco plants fill the air especially white ones, and some phlox is still out. A last little bit of summer jasmine can still take one's breath away. Now I am by my back door where my Ionicera honeys the yard and there is another more insistent smell for I am hungry and have not got dinner ready. It is the smell of someone else's dinner. September has become warm and summery enough again for people to open their windows on to the balmy evening to get the refreshment of the fragrance-loaded air from the garden, and my nose and taste buds are reacting to the savours of their good cooking coming across into my yard.

Mid-September turns wet and cold and I am not ready for warmer clothes, for an indoor life, for the blocking of activity from the senses, especially smell, because of catarrhs and phlegms. These, as well as the disappearance of sun and warmth, may be contributing to flowers smelling less.

While so many flowers are going to seed and dying down, some of the daisy family are coming into their own: Michaelmas daisies, chrysanthemums pre-eminent. There is a lovely yellow and the tighter florets of a rust-coloured one, stronger-smelling in the wet like a thick short-haired dog's coat. The odour of chrysanthemums, which D. H. Lawrence so disliked, mingles with the continuing dahlias, nasturtiums and calendula. The strongest smell you get from the dahlia is acrid on your fingers when you are dead-heading, pulling off the squelchy brown remains of a flowerhead or picking off the slug-riddled leaves. All these flowers, but particularly calendula that, in keeping with its name, thrives during nearly every month of the calendar, easily transfer their acrid smell which refreshes some people and sickens others, to hands that brush petals or pick off leaves or touch stems. With feverfew, you do not need to rub the leaves or fondle the bright white buttons of its daisy or pull off dead leaves and stems to receive its refreshing pungency, nor those of the delicate menthol-scented geranium. I have small pots of these here and there in yard and on beds so that I can bring them in when frost threatens, as they are not hardy. Mingled with these strong smells, there is a faint honey smell from some tall yellow daisies within reach of my nosing their cool petals and hairy brown centres, something I cannot do with the huge sunflowers way above my head. They are beginning to hang their heavy heads and should be dripping with nectar. Their great plates of seed-heads look a bit like honeycombs.

As if to soften the oranges and yellows and pungent smells of these flowers, there are softer pink-mauve ones. A flourishing tall clump of Japanese anemones has established itself in front of banks of montbretia entrenched against the wall. Their deep red-orange slashes against green-ribbon spears of leaves are brighter than ever this year. They have no scent (at least, not to my nose at this time), nor do the low mallow flowers whose thick dark green leafage leads one to expect a sappy smell. Two flowers in the same colour range, whose sudden emergence from the earth at this time always gives me a delightful surprise, are my miniature cyclamen which carpet increasing patches under a japonica bush on the raised bed outside my back door. I never believe my experience that they do not smell, they *look* so scented; but I have not been able to establish the scented variety, and mine that are keeping their fragrance to themselves, do well.

The yellow fruit of the japonica bush, whose orange flowers had not much scent to my nose, are beginning to drop and even just picking them up releases an exquisite piquant spicy appley smell. How much more so when, next month, I shall be cutting and cooking them to make quince jam and jelly. This is also the time when, picking up windfalls from my cooking apple tree at the bottom of the garden, I may get the blessing of the sudden appearance of colchicum. Now, they *do* have a sweet honey smell. It is not as free on the air as that first note of fragrance in early spring, like the call of a woodwind instrument or a bird, when the clump of early pale mauve crocus have opened in unison, almost with a ping at the summons of the first late morning strength of the spring sun. Kneeling on the damp grass, I have sometimes got a waft from the autumn one that has been worth it, but alas the slugs find all parts of this plant particularly succulent and my delight at the flower's dramatic appearance can be short lived. There can quickly be no trace of them at all, and one has to imagine hard to guess where they have been.

The touch of the rain is enough to bring the pungency out of the leaves and twigs and stems which, as the season progresses, are increasingly the loci for fragrance and aroma: blackcurrant always, rosemary, lavender, marjoram, mint; picking off the seed heads of calendula is stronger than smelling the flower, the leaves are always pungent. Stocks are still sweet, alyssum smells if you sniff it close to but it is more bitter now. A few sweet peas are still out and a faint trace from one or two solitary florets of phlox among the clusters of brown seed heads, but the scent from these is mainly imaginary now. Powdery-blue clumps of one of my favourite edging plants, ageratum, are still in flower. I have never detected a scent from these flowers through all the months they have been flowering, but rub the thick dark green leaves and pull off the browned seed heads and you will get a very sharp astringent smell.

In succession, I trail my hand (carefully) across juniper, low on a wall, and mint in a nook under it. I am coming back up my garden path from the back gate to the yard and back door. I am by the patch of chamomile I had recently clipped. I find its sweet smell a little sickly close to. I prefer the appley smell of the wild rayless mayweed that grows on cart tracks and hard-baked trodden field edges and cracks in pavements but which I have never succeeded in getting to grow in the cracks in my path, where all sorts of things lodge and thrive happily without my welcoming them. My blackcurrant bush is near to the chamomile and, as at any season, leaf and stem release at a touch their strong unique smell.

At ankle-level on my right, winter savory is in flower, then comes my thyme, practically a bush by now, which flowered last month. My lavender is grey again; I clipped away most of the second lot of flowering stalks which I'd left for the bees when I made my first cut, just before the flowers were fully out. Apparently, lavender retains and exudes its scent longest if you pick it just before its flowers open, but I find lavender lasts at whatever stage you pick it. When the flowers are over, scent still comes from the twiggy bushes. It stays a long time on my skin, oily from rubbing stalk and seed head between my fingers.

I brush past my rosemary, grown into a small tree now and part of the hedge between neighbour and me. One of the reasons I let this vigorous, quite prickly, potentially painful bush grow inconveniently is that if you have to push past it you will release, in all weathers, in all seasons, but particularly when the raindrops from it trickle down your neck and obscure your vision by sluicing your glasses, the most refreshing sympathetic aroma. The green lanterns of the hop flower that seemed to glimmer in the dusk are black now that it is night. They are beginning to exude the garlicky smell which will be really strong when they have shrivelled and dried to brown. A honeysuckle has flowered at last after years of prolific green leaf, and on this night it seems that the scent of that one flower is enough to fill the garden.

Many bushes and plants still have flowers coming while some others are turning to berry and seed head. At this time, I have berry and flower of cotoneaster, honeysuckle, bramble and my white rugosa rose bush, whose second and even third flowering I have managed to prolong by taking off the hips as soon as they form (and not waiting for them to ripen into gleaming orangey-red, for by then the bush is so pretty again I would not like to spoil it). By now, all but the occasional late still strongly sweet flowers have disappeared, the light red of the fruit is turning darker and softer. Picking off one or two of these to find out if they smelt of roses, they squished in my fingers giving off a mouth-watering smell of peach. Perhaps I should try and use these large hips to make rose-hip syrup instead of the ones I gather later in the year from the hedges?

Even the berries and seed heads that do not give off a fragrance (and most fruits do have a scent) recall the scents of the flowers they have come from. I am picking off pods and seed heads to dry and store, and as I shove them in my pocket I vow I will go in straightaway and find an envelope or container and write the name of what, where and when. Emptying the pockets of old trousers or skirt for the wash, I often come across a silt of fluff, crumbs of soil, bits of stalk or husk and seeds embedded in the seams. My pockets have never actually grown flowers or parsnips but I did notice the other day that an onion discarded in a bowl in which I'd left some rag had spread tough white roots through the fabric and had produced a bright green shoot.

The seeds and the bulbs we either buy at this time or retrieve from those dug up and saved earlier, give us the promise of scent. It is a forward whiff which is to cross the coming months of dark damp enclosed dulled air, like a ray of light hitting a mirror in a darkened room, and transport us the other side of winter to spring. They hold future scents, literally, in their fabric, as well as in our imagination. September is one of the fulcrums of the year, balancing summer passed with winter to come.

October

The last quarter of our year is made up of the fire months, culminating, of course, in the fire festival at the winter solstice, the festival which is the symbol of light and life flaming from the nadir, from the shrivelled centre of the dying world.

October begins this phase. The lighting of fires is not its first aspect, although even in a mild October there can be sudden sharp frosts. The smell of smoke one used to get, going home down any street at dusk, then dark, as the evenings drew in, changed very recognizably from the bonfires of early autumn to smoke from house fires. Aromas of pungency and sweetness from bonfires drift waywardly through the still afternoon, their source unlocated behind wall or in paddock – a woody, resinous sometimes fruity sort of smell, sappy and vegetable. The slow steady column of smoke from chimneys is visible in the dusk once one's nose has detected the more chemical tarry whiff of coal. Sometimes a lighter column moves against a cloudy sky, on clear nights more defined, until it spreads and dissipates into the air, as the vapour trail of an aeroplane shoots across the blue does, its straight white ribbon, made dazzling by the gold light, gradually breaking up until it is indistinguishable from the wispy little pufflets of a summer dawn. In the same way, the locatable smell of a coal fire is suffused through the atmosphere and becomes a redolence in the evening dusk that draws one indoors to comfort and warmth.

The fire that October first brings to me, though, is what has started in September. It is the woods flaming; not the terrifying summer fires in some afforested countries, but the fire with no heat, no destruction. The torch that sets fire to our woods, hedges, trees in roads and gardens, blazing through cool damp darkening days is the sap withdrawing. It is a dying that can make us gasp at the intensity and great range of colour, as wonderstruck as when we are taken breathless by the bursting open of gorgeous flowers.

Apart from the fact that at this time we accelerate artificially the advance of night into the afternoon, the further north you live the quicker the pace of the lengthening and shortening of days. Length of the hours of light more than temperature affects the growth of plants, and I have seen trees by street lamps full of green leaves when others in the same road are brown and bare.

It is at the end of October that the most important flower of the autumn (for some people, the most important of all flowers) comes to its eminence. The chrysanthemum is of a large family, and some flower through the summer. For me, chrysanthemum means the autumn. There are two varieties I am fondest of. One is the spray, the other is the great many-petalled luscious head in whose cool refreshing odour you can bury your face, the sort that looks almost edible, like a succulent mop-head cabbage.

I knew someone once, banned at intervals from a cosy little pub in Maida Vale (when that area was not what it is today) who, at a certain stage in the evening took to chewing one of the three very fine chrysanthemum heads – a yellow, a bronze, a white – that were usually in a vase on the bar. Perhaps it was like a cat chewing grass to right its digestive system. I don't think it would have occurred to him to buy chrysanthemums, as one might buy fruit, from a stall. It must have been when they were in a vase, their redolence being brought out by the beery, smoky warmth of the snug, that they exercised their irresistible fascination on him.

The chrysanthemum, rather like the rose, has had much symbolic life attached to it over the centuries. It has come, fairly late in its mythical history, to be associated by some with death. All Saints' Day falls on 1 November. It is the Christian ceremony when, particularly in France, families bring flowers to the graves of relatives and remember their dead. Naturally they bring what is in season at the time and this is, above all, the chrysanthemum. It has become the flower you take to the dead because it is available; not obtained or grown especially because it has some religious significance. In a much earlier civilization, this gorgeous flower was used in religious ceremonies and art to symbolize life but because it has for Christian centuries been used as a message between the living and the dead, a certain amount of superstition has become attached to people's reactions to it. In France, apparently, at least among those who understand the etiquettes of visiting, it would be a social gaffe of the most tactless sort to present one's hostess with chrysanthemums; worse, probably, than bringing no flowers at all.

For those who do not like the odour of chrysanthemuns, their reaction is probably reinforced by its association with death, with wakes, with visits to cemeteries on bleak wet windy Sundays, and it is a very pervasive smell. I myself love it. Perhaps this is because the astringent smells of autumn suit me, but my partiality for dahlias and chrysanthemums may stem from a bus ride on a dark foggy autumn evening more than fifty years ago.

When I was about sixteen, I went for a time to school in Oxford where I stayed the week, coming home to Buckinghamshire by bus every Friday evening for the weekend. By the time we reached Stokenchurch, where I got off and waited for another bus, it would be dark. The dark foggy damp nights are the ones I remember. One particularly raw night, when the bus stopped on the unlit road going between dark fields, a countrywoman got on, fresh-coloured cheeks and round face pleasant with smiles. She had a large wicker basket full of flowers which were dewy and wet from the damp air as was her hair and coat. She exchanged pleasantries with the driver and others of the regulars, speaking with the lovely soft Oxford county accent very different from Oxford town. I suppose I must have been staring at the flowers, not meaning to be rude or draw attention to myself, but literally feasting my eyes on the colours and my nose on the freshness of the fragrance that had suddenly blazed out of the dark and cold. I daresay she asked me if I liked flowers, and told me they were from her garden. They were great lavish dahlias and chrysanthemums. I may have seen her once more and then not, although I always looked for her to emerge from the dark roadside onto the lighted bus with her cornucopia.

In my memory of my idea of my life at that time, she figures more importantly than people I saw every day. Of course, my memory of those times has crystallised them into a fiction. Those sort of journeys, possibly the very road itself, do not exist now, but the flowers, almost a symbol for something ephemeral, perishable, whose very flourishing means the ending of their short life, are still here, the same and with exactly the same existence and function. And I am still drawn by the cool and flamboyant life of them and by their refreshing smell.

October is a pretty month, and although there are flowers blooming apart from chrysanthemums, most of its glories and delights are of leaves, of fruit, of harvest. Our perceptions are drawn to trees and hedgerow life, our noses to the earth and to the floors of woods, to canal side, river bank and ditches. October smells of digging up roots, of walking through leaves in woods. Leaves are drifted into piles or banks, or are raked up, and then sometimes scattered by wind or children shuffling through them. Even adults still enjoy doing this, turning over the leaf-mould, releasing a nutty savoury healthy aroma. There are some faint roses. There are still stocks. If the morning is shrouded in mist, you may get a sight of what for me is the definitive mark of the arrival of autumn – shawls of beaded moisture the spiders have hung over a dense evergreen hedge, in my case a yew hedge that grows down the right-hand side of my yard.

The early days of October are often wonderfully sunlit, a blue and gold air. The fruit of my orange japonica ripens to yellow. I pick up the fallen quinces which, when cut and cooked, will have a sharp appley smell with a clove background. Even now, the smooth cool skin against my nose gives off a hint. Next month I shall pick them from the branches which grow against a wall, leaving the fruit I can't reach as decoration: yellow globes growing through the cotoneaster that clads the grey stone with its green branches spread like a fan and studded with masses of tight orange-red berries like beads.

Menthol-scented geranium is in flower and this delicate white tiny-petalled scrap gives off a pungent aroma even before being touched, as do the soft grey-green rounded leaves. It clears the head better than any precious (pricey) little brown glass bottle from the health shop, and even the twiggy bits of dead leaf act in this way and keep their strength for weeks. The delicate rose-coloured cyclamen, whose thick leafage comes out later, has a long flowering period but no smell; at the same time, the green spears of the grape hyacinth are coming up in thick clumps. In spite of the promise of a prolific honey smell next year from them I am uneasy that they are shooting so early. The greeny-white star of a few astrantia flowers among their browning yellowing leaves give off a faint fragrance if you smell close, the leaves giving off a slight pleasantly acrid smell when crushed.

I miss the extension of the long summer evening, but one exceptionally warm night at the beginning of the month I go out to empty the teapot and then down the sheltered path on to the open grass beyond my shed. I was beginning to forget the extension of night, getting used, before I needed to, to thinking the day finishes when the light goes. Oenothera is still opening, the stocks still sending out dizzy pleasure with their strong sweet clove smell. The tobacco plants that are still flowering are scented now it is dark. Sweet peas are over but masses of white dahlias and chrysanthemums are coming into their own, and the calendula leaves have a fresh pungency. I bend to the herbs. I touch the leaves, but there is a light garlic smell strong on the air coming from the shed roof. The translucent green hops which have grown over it are turning to redolent papery brown husks. They are at their most savoury when they have dried to the brittleness of insect wings. I empty the teapot on to some stock plants which ought to have been planted out long ago, and hear the owl.

Hedgerow and field smells, the rather acrid smells of autumn – late blackberries going soft and mouldy, and sloe berries turning, the smell of nuts and roots and rot in the woods and dingles, the bees in the ivy – these are taking over from the flower scents. The wisping cotton of wild clematis seed head is beginning to clad all the hedges where earlier the sweet smell of the flower was among the heady benefits of hedgerow-gathering walks. The seed heads are very tickly to the nose and it is not only a remembered scent it produces, but sneezes.

Ageratum must be the longest-lasting flower in my garden, but it is at its end now and the ice plant with its pretty red-pink cushion of a flower is coming into its best. It, too, has a slightly hairy smell when damp, not really particular to itself as a flower, more like damp cloth. The succulence of its light grey-green fleshy leaves, if snapped, just smell of green juiciness to me.

The tall yellow daisies with brown centres looking over the fence have a faint honey smell in the sun if smelt close to, but watch it! for late bees are still active in the extended warmth. They make for stray lavender flowers that are still opening among the grey stalks and seed heads. Everything about the lavender always smells, the grey-green new leaves beginning to grow after the cutting, the grey stalks and seed heads, the last stray flowers opening to the warm late season. There is alyssum out still and it gives off its scent, but not so sweet. The fever-few is flowering, clumps of candid white buttons. Every part of this plant is aromatic but its particular astringency is in the leaves, with a slightly bitter back-kick, refreshing for those with an aquired taste for it. The leaves are the part you eat (although probably eating the flower would do you no harm). A leaf of feverfew turns a marmite sandwich into something quite special. There are flowers again on my rosemary bush for its second season, its thick-needled branches growing upward like candelabra. All parts of this plant exude a pungent aroma into the air.

There is still some flower on a large clover I let grow on the edge of a border, but the scent of high summer clover has gone. Honeysuckle still has some flowers among the berries which have been bright and ripening for some time. You have to search for or imagine scent from these plants, but calendula and nasturtium, both leaf and flower, give out their strength and claim the nose's attention, as do sage, lemon balm, the dead heads and stalks of dahlias, and comfrey when you crush or pull its sappy leaves or stalks. The sap has a cool light summery cucumbery smell and it reminds me of witch hazel. (This may be imaginary as I know both are good for bruises. Witch hazel is one of my favourite smells whether from a bottle or a plant.) Wear gloves for tidying up your comfrey plants, and feeding your compost with the leaves and stalks, because they are very scratchy.

Pansies are having a new lease of life, particularly those I got round to dead-heading, trimming the dying stalks, but they do not have much scent, straggling up cool and moist from the overcrowding growth in the flower beds. I pick a few of those delicately petalled upturned faces, that feel restorative to my skin and lips as I brush them lightly across my face. When I get back inside as an evening shower closes off a bright blowy day, I find their frail stalks tight in my hand. I put them in an egg cup of water with a floret of alyssum. They revive later and when I hold the egg cup to my nose, I do get a faint sweet smell from them, reminding me of earlier in the year when it mingled in the perfumed air of the garden. Wild strawberries are still fruiting and their fragrant sharpness on the tongue also recalls the scents of summer, though they were sweeter then.

I have also picked two scraps of plant whose scent persists: some leaves of my purple sage for a gargle for a sore throat, and the last few florets of my white phlox which, if you pick at the right time, retains its haunting whiff of spice for years (literally), even when reduced by much fingering to a brown dusty scrap no more substantial than a flake of skin in a bowl or pot with other dry leaves.

There are warm dawdling days after the briskness of a light frost. Autumn crocus is opening in the sun with a delicate sweet smell, and in extended warmth a late sunflower. Ivy, which I dislike – every part of it: root, clutching stem, shiny acrid leaves, heavily scented flowers – is prolific in scent now, and attracting a frenzy of activity among insects. It is a pity I am prejudiced against it as it has many attributes I might like in other plants. It is associated for me forever with mustiness and stifling decay and ruin, with dark stench and something wrong, more than the gloom of woods. To counter it on walks, there is the smell of beech mast underfoot and sweet and spicy smoke from bonfires.

Pre-eminent among strong recognizable smells of plants grown for food is every part of the tomato. You may be picking late-ripening fruit, or green ones before the frost, or pulling up and burning finished or rotting stems. If there are some still alive and fruiting, you can carefully ease up the roots and hang the whole plant up by its root in a shed – the 'airy dry shed', beloved of advisors, in which to store onions, corms, bulbs, seeds, apples, potatoes. The envigorating strong earthy tomato root and leaf smell is a good addition to the atmosphere of your shed, if the other things in it (like hammock cushions and old blankets for picnics) are not going mouldy in the dark damp corner you slung them in, having dashed out through a sudden thunderstorm on an August day to rescue all the equipment of an outdoor life the settled hot summer days had lulled us into thinking was ours forever.

October harvesting smells are largely to do with what we dig up and store, not smells from the fields as we walk or ride by, whether it be potatoes, carrots, turnips, or the roots and tubers of perennials that are not hardy, like dahlias and begonias, or clumps we want to divide or restrict from taking over the whole of the bed they're in – in my case just now, day lilies, montbretia and the like.

What does the rough wind bring in October, seeming to come fitfully from far, from dark days in other places that have not yet reached us? It is this smell of the earth, with the fruits of the earth we are digging up out of it, mixed with what is going down into it: the leaves and stalks from tree, bush and plant, fruit dropping and rotting, innumerable berries, seeds and pulpy fruits containing seeds: acorns and rose hips, sycamore wings and ash keys, apples, nightshade, plums.

So the cutting back, digging, digging up, transplanting that can begin in October as sap withdraws from plants, releases the October smells as much as the rain and the wind, when they come, draw them out from the plants that are still flowering. Increasingly from this time, the smells from what we have grown outside will be released indoors. In spring and summer, the fragrance in the air of vegetable matter growing is really for insects. Our use of it (apart from enjoyments not to do with eating) – cooking, seething, jamming, preserving, storing – moves the aromas inside the house. Added to the smell of the cooking of apple ginger may be the tart fresh one of green tomatoes sliced and spread on a dish under salt in preparation for green tomato chutney.

November

Much of November belies the dread attached to its reputation, the shutting down, the gloom, the fog, the dark wet, the cold and the 'colds', autumn shrinking down into winter.

It can be pretty. While golden and russet leaves are still falling, making there seem to be fires on the ground in woods as well as on the crests of the trees, branches that are still green may be silvered with frost on high open land. As the sun strengthens on such a morning, one side of a hedge may be dark, clotted with little chunks of ice and the other bright with colour that seems to drip off it as the sun rainbows the thaw. It can be warm, it can be vigorous, as much of a mixture as May, its counterpart on the opposite side of the seasons' clock.

Whatever its weather, though, it is the time when the dark draws in quickly, when more of our life, and its smells, goes on inside buildings. We are more aware of the smells of the house and, even when we are out, the smells we notice are from places we take shelter in – cafés, pubs, shops, cinemas, all those 'indoor' places we go 'out' to, to work, get and spend in, to meet people, to enjoy ourselves.

We are plunged doubly into the dark in November from our habit of 'putting the clocks back' at the end of October, so that even when the weather is mild, life for most of us suddenly moves indoors. This choosing of November to 'begin winter time' is a man-made division, but not all that recent, for 31 October was the last day of the Celtic year.

We should by now have got the toys of summer packed away unless they're already rusted and rotted to the point we might as well leave them as depressing marks of winter's (ie our) inertia. Before we get too used to not budging from the fire in the evenings until we go to bed, we will have a session in the loft to look through stored produce and bring down some of those winter clothes we shall be needing which we were so pleased we could put away – oh, so long ago it now seems, when we never wanted to see them again but only wear light cotton.

A friend said to me the other day, 'Didn't you love the smell going up into the apple loft as a child and seeing the apples laid out in rows?' Well, no, my loft is not really that sort. It may be 'frost free and airy' (desirable conditions mentioned in advice on storing); unfortunately not free of other things. In spite of there being no visible trace of pets in the spaces from floor to ceiling in my rooms, the rest of the house provides – as we are told large trees do – a habitat that supports a variety of wildlife species. In this way, the house is like the body, say the gut, which provides for and needs hundreds, probably thousands of germs to keep it going, which works well as long as they keep to their place.

I don't mind being host to insects, rodents, grubs, worms, caterpillars, beetles, woodlice *et al* if only they would keep to their part of the building, that is between floor-boards and ceiling below, and within walls. In a good system, from what I've tried to learn from books and experts about the natural world, all these living things live off each other, keeping a balance, and are too fly to destroy their own home (in this case my home, too). I suppose the spiders do eat the flies, but the rest live off what I provide in the way of books, blankets, clothes, suitcases, carpets, stacks of papers, rolls of wallpaper, feather pillows, old leather briefcases, pictures, mattresses, tablecloths, cardboard boxes (some venerable enough for museums and inherited, along with bad habits, from an ancestral hoarder), bundles of notebooks, offcuts of wood, lagging, crates of old brown envelopes full of letters, cards, pro-, grammes, bank books, gas and electricity bills, plastic bags full of ditto. At this time, however, there are also thick brown paper bags of potatoes, boxes of apples each wrapped in newspaper, onions hanging in nets by the window, which I remind myself is what I've come up here to check.

The aroma you would encounter trying to get up the stairs into my loft between stacks of books varies. Sometimes it is sweet and fruity, sometimes it is bad and fruity. I will spare those of you who have not had to deal with hidden corpses of mice and the resulting miasma, further nosmic details.

Although we are indoors more, there is a restlessness to these first days of early dark. Something is going on with the weather high up above the curtain of night. The wind may change direction, then veer north, bringing a sudden short clatter of sleet onto the leaves it is swirling in eddies against our gates and walls, and then clear to soft blue greyness and shafts of pale sunlight again.

There is the feeling of something impending. It is a time of expectation, wanting something to prepare for. Advent, of course. *Advenire* – to happen, to come about. The Christian calendar has taken advantage of what the body naturally reacts to in our climate.

For many, the dominant aromas are from consolations for our poor sore throats and clogged sinuses and heavy heads: hot toddies, menthol, linctus, lemon and honey, Friar's and other balsams, astringent antiseptic gargles, fumigations and disinfectants to counter the phlegms and hawking, the trumpetings and croaking and complainings of a family with a cold.

I knew a family, teetotal down four generations, who never partook of so much as half a glass of cooking sherry at Christmas or a glass of Champagne at weddings. In their kitchen on the mantelpiece, along with the tin of tea, salt, pepper etc, were two half-empty bottles of thick dark brown liquid. Remembering Alice and the little bottle with such dire consequences of her greed, I opened it and sniffed gingerly. The smell was delicious, a mixture from which I detected something like cinnamon, dark treacle, something hot, something soothing. I could not but taste this elixir and only my adherence to the Norwegian Hut Principle enabled me to resist addicton. Apparently, the matriarch of this family, against all drugs, never taking pain-killers, got through a great deal of this cough mixture, especially made up for her according to an old recipe. It was, of course, addictive and I for one was glad she could enjoy that calmative and delicious odour with a quiet conscience. So when you are making a healthy hot drink for a poor fellow sufferer, be lavish with the cinnamon, the nutmeg and the cloves.

Days before the end of October, what pervaded the air was not only the normal smell of garden bonfires but fireworks, their more chemical whiff tingling in the nose through the smell of fire. There is a charring, a metal gunpowdery tang in the air, and if it is dank and misty you will get it on your tongue, too.

It used to be all saved up for Guy Fawkes night – what children could collect with their old push chair, or a box on wheels, containing the gross masked doll who was their Guy. They would station him at strategic places to intercept passers-by or shoppers or men going into or coming out of the pub on Thursday or Friday evenings. The experienced ones didn't bother those going in but waited for them as they came out, relaxed, generous and sentimental. A day or two before the 5th, there might be a few bangers set off in the day to annoy cyclists and frighten younger siblings and dogs and friends. Dusk at that time always smelled smokey and there were, of course, quite a few practise bonfires and the sound of fire engines. The presence of carbon in the night air probably was a component in the increased excitement we breathed in on those mild invigorating evenings coming home to tea from work or school through the early dark. The shops were still open and lit up and the streets crowded but fireworks were not generally sold much before the end of October. Once the pennies you'd managed to get from going out early with your Guy were spent, that was it, you didn't (couldn't) just go and ask for more.

When you go out into your garden a day or two after your bonfire party, what will you find apart from a noseful of damp char, soggy paper wrappings and a pan with dirty cold fat solidifying round small lumps of burnt offerings smelling so different from the night of the party when mouthwatering wafts of fresh sausages cooking had suffused the air of the neighbourhood? The sausages had been bedded in floury white potatoes, skins baked to crispness with the resinous wood of the fire they were baked in acting as condiment. Perhaps you will unearth the carving fork you had out there for turning the sausages and haven't seen since?

There may be autumn crocus out, stock still flowering and fragrant, ageratum, antirrhinum, alyssum, roses still, and some budding again, and a late clematis. Calendula and feverfew still have strong scent.

Pulling up beansticks to clear the wigwams round which the dried beige stalks of the dead runners are shrinking, I get the pungency of roots and disturbed earth. The flourishing weeds are almost cress-like in their crisp green, for we have had plenty of mild wet weather to extend the growing season. Dianthus and lobelia continue in sheltered places in the garden, although there is no smell from dianthus now and never from lobelia. There might be a last dahlia or two if there hasn't been a frost and there is always a freshness off them. The odour of chrysanthemums lingers as they gleam, or peer through the thick air of a misty morning, or a foggy dusk.

The smell from the hedges is cold and dark and bitter. Driving or walking on some dim blanketed morning, you might feel you have got into the set of a ghoulish film where an ancient ruined forest surrounding the haunted castle is festooned in old murky cobwebs, or Miss Haversham's room where no breath of air has disturbed the clinging grey skeins of the spiders for decades. The old man's beard is dense and greyer and more stifling, coating bushes and even some trees along the sides of the roads for miles. At other times when the sun may be clearing the air, I have thought 'We have had a frost' and that it is the light on it that is brightening and whitening the edges of the woods until, looking closer, I see it is the wild clematis' final cling.

By now, even when leaf fall is late, canals and pools or boggy patches in woods, inlets and cuttings in river banks will begin to smell more of whatever is settling and silting and rotting down in the lower layers of the water, much of it vegetation, sometimes human rubbish. It is this ooze, enriched by what is laid down in autumn, with which floods in February may coat and slime embankments, paths, streets, and houses. What should really be left to rot and disperse under water does indeed smell foul when impregnated in sodden carpets and upholstery and smeared on walls. But the muddy water-weedy, leaf-rot sort of smell is pleasant and interesting if the water you are by in a warm November is not too stagnant, but quiet enough to let the life in it mature at its own pace. The nose is careful at such times, guarding the stomach against anything too nauseous, for the sensitivity of the nose is just as much a warning system to aid our survival as the sensitivity of our finger-tips.

There will be the smell of apples, potatoes, beetroot, parsnips, leeks, onions, tomatoes as you gather and lift, store, cook and eat them. There will be the smell of cooking coming from houses when someone in a steamy kitchen opens a window for a short time to clear the air, there will be crowded pubs spilling out tobacco smoke and odours of drink and food; the smell of fish and chips frying, billowing out into the dark street as people push in from the cold, opening the steamed-up door, or come out with their packages redolent of oil and vinegar. This latter smell is particularly nauseating when part of the morning-after rubbish mingling with the contents of acrid ashtrays emptied out the door of the pub by the barman as he locks up for the night. But if you are picking your way down the street early on a 'morning-after' and pass a bakery you might get a comforting, reviving whiff from the bread baking.

I travelled home one sombre afternoon two-thirds of the way through November when rain returning after a bright pretty morning brought the dark down even sooner than the clock did. It was too wet and dark to go down the garden to see how the remaining flowers were being obscured and drawn down by the approach of winter, but from the bathroom window the cotoneaster over the wall on the left and another one fanning out against the yew hedge on the right had suddenly become a blush of red. The remaining berries were not visibly separate from the stippling of small dense leaves whose dark green gloss had earlier set off the berries' red, for the leaves had become all orange-red like a fire-flush against grey wall and dark yew.

As I turned to go out into the pouring rain to bring in the last bit of luggage from the car, a sweet whiff of early summer crossed the damp air suffused with diesel and muck from the road, and the dank smell of the shut, unheated house. It was from a pot of paper-white narcissi, jonquils I had bought in flower from a shop. I had put this pot on a stool in the hall, the only available place not covered with luggage and bundles and bags of supplies.

I usually like things in season, flowering at a time they can look after themselves outdoors, but spring in winter and 'present laughter' as well as anticipatory pleasures, are good for us, and hyacinths, to me almost a symbol of April, in pots indoors are also part of Christmas. Now these fragrant narcissi unnaturally, almost artificially, are cleansing away the smell of dank air imprisoned in the house with the breath of their fragrance.

It was also when travelling one November day, lowering the car window to let in mild blustery fresh air, that there came with it the nutty smell of woods and leaf-mould and wet, and then suddenly and long forgotten, the smell from the brewery sweet and malty for several yards. I was whizzing past at 70 mph but the smell lasted and seemed to travel with the car a little way. The last time I'd smelt it, it was accompanied by cut grass and the two had mingled, the one not unlike the other, warm and almost animal, a whiff of horses. This time the grass was dank and sodden and the fields turned into marsh or lakes, but the smell of brewing cut across clear and clean, solacing and invigorating to the nose, as the various effusions after beer has been drunk are not. In the same way, even to an addict, the actual cup of coffee you drink never sends you to that realm of pleasure that passing a shop where coffee is being roasted and ground can do.

December

If you are 'not doing Christmas' (the message I give out at this time),
there is a great deal to enjoy before the shutdown you're working your
way towards brings its peaceful lull, when the state of the ground will
make work outside impossible, when there is no post to look for, no
shopping to be done.

December is often milder than March. The miraculous flowering of dead
branches used as a symbol in the Christian story has a counterpart in
botanical accounts of everyday miracles. The Christmas Day report from
Kew Gardens has more than once mentioned that the prunus was
flowering.

There is more activity in plants than people who are immured in shops, offices and houses during reduced daylight hours have the opportunity to notice. There are winter-flowering shrubs that may be budding now: sarcococca which keeps its glossy dark green leaves all year, flower buds on the bare branches of *Daphne mezereum*, on dead-looking twigs of *Hamamelis mollis*.

Fragrance outdoors in this season is not so much a twinkle in the eye as a sniff in the nosmic imagination. You might find a very early snow-drop, but there will be no scent from it until warmth opens it. You will see the tips of bulbs and look forward to being overcome by spring.

Flower scents are future pleasures but in a mild, still, early December, perhaps on a day recovering from dark wild weather but not yet bound by frost, you might be getting a load of manure on to your patch.

However much you dislike dung squelched onto your shoes, or matted into your dog's fur after a joyous (to the dog) roll on a wet walk across fields, it will smell good to you when rotting down on your ground. The warm redolence in the steam that rises as it's tipped out is a stimulation. The carting and the digging will warm us up on those drear days when we feel too low to leave a warm house, or relish much inside it, and the manure will warm up the earth it is dug into.

It is steam that carries – outdoors through damp air, indoors permeating heated houses – the smells of Christmas.

'Not doing Christmas' releases mid-December for joining in other people's preparations, for taking part in the life of the town, for parties, for perhaps a rare prolonged lunch with friends one meets on one of the days when offices are still open and the 'working world' is taking advantage of last opportunities before family bosoms expand and enwrap its members for the holiday.

Market stalls smell more luxurious at Christmas time. Come-hitherish steam rises from a bucket of mulled wine the fishmonger is warming up his customers with while they wait for their fish to be gutted by hands reddened and swollen with cold. To go with the warming drink, perhaps we will have a taste of that rich ripe cheese signalling from a stall nearby.

The fruit stall has exotic fruits, sometimes with a sample cut open to show its ripeness and fragrance. Who would put up with bottled lime juice now that we can get fresh limes? There is the acquired rather turpentiny taste of the mango, the sweet gut-soothing flesh, dripping with juice, of papaya, the unique perfume of the pineapple. There are salads, expensive but necessary at this time of year, tarter, bitterer tastes to counteract all the sweetness, the dripping fat roasts, the cream: peppery watercress, endive, chicory, and pungent strange fungi like distorted ear-lobes as well as the more familiar smell of mushrooms, invigorating like a well-dug manured bed of earth. There are smooth purple figs on the twig as well as powdery dried ones; dates, the fragrance of sweet grapes and the more sugary aroma from the boxes of raisins and sultanas. All this mingles with the more usual fruit and veg smells: different sorts of apples, pears, carrots, parsnips, swedes, potatoes, sprouts pre-eminent among cabbages and greens. Surely it's the smell which accounts for people enjoying buying produce more in an open-air market than in refrigerated supermarkets?

Lastly, and to me firstly and mainly and chiefly, a redolence, hovering through the build-up to Christmas, lingering afterwards and back through all the years: the smell of oranges.

It is Christmas Eve. I have had a nice day doing a few errands before the shut-down, relaxed in anticipation of a self-indulgent week, salved by shared goodwill and generosity. 'See you in the New Year,' I say to them all.

I have cleaned out and laid the fire in the upstairs sitting-room, polished the fender and candlesticks, found the candles, unpacked the bags of fruit and put it in bowls, got a double issue of the *Radio Times*, put my current pile of books, pen and writing paper on a table I have cleared of all else save a bottle of very good sherry I was given, a glass and a plate of mince pies (bought not made). I will light the fire when I'm ready to sit down.

Steam from some smoked haddock I am poaching to make a kedgeree that will last me for days has dulled the kitchen window. All I can see in it is a vague figure and dim shapes moving. The smell of the fish and the steaming rice, the cut hard-boiled egg and the chopped parsley, a resinous smell on my hands from the kindling wood, the smell of hot mince pies mingling with dry sherry, candles and the fruit I have put in bowls – these smells have taken me back . . . and back to Christmas Eves when I used to cook food anyone could eat at any time, as they came in and out shopping, seeing friends or stopping to chat and sample and 'help' in the kitchen, or put up decorations or whisper noisily over conspiratorial packaging. It became a custom to have fish. It was cheaper than meat then, although smoked haddock was quite a treat for us, and we were going, unaccustomedly, to have a great deal of meat the next day, for which we were now preparing stuffings and sauces and accompaniments. I would hardly sit down or have time to change all week.

The shapes the steam is swirling about in the window clarify: someone is holding up a bowl. 'The fridge is full, where shall I put the trifle, shouldn't it be somewhere cool?' Someone else pushes into the kitchen with a bulky clanking bag. 'Not on the pastry', I shout. 'There isn't room in here', but ginger beer for shandy, a package of chips, and a bottle of olives are plonked down. Someone steps on a bag of crisps and giggles at the explosion. The television has been turned on, loud. I am about to call up the stairs for it to be turned down when, 'Come on,' they yell, 'they're doing a repeat of The Two Ronnies. We'll do that for you later.' 'Take a plate', I shout after the retreating chip papers dripping grease, and the slopping glasses, 'I've *cleaned* up there.' 'We'll clean up again afterwards. Come on, it's starting. It's your favourite. You know you want to watch it.'

We light the fire and the candles and drink fizz and sherry and eat chips and mince pies, and get greasy and I put oranges by the fire to warm which brings out their scent and taste, and they squirt juice all over the place when we peel them.

The steam is clearing now, only steaming up my spectacles a little as I put out a plateful of food. I shall eat it upstairs by the fire. The kitchen is clear, the table scrubbed, on it no large fowl to be stuffed, thank goodness, no bowls of fat, jugs of stock. The house is clean and warm and quiet, the only noise coming from the road outside. My house is right on the road. Often when someone slams a car door, it sounds as if it's inside. There are doors slamming, people calling to each other, laughter, children shouting, a tooting of horns, shouted greetings. How nice that everyone's enjoying themselves, I think as I check that the gas taps are off and turn the light out on the kitchen. It is calm and resting, ready for the new year, as I make for my own luxurious evening by the fire.

There is a bump as I reach the stairs, then a bang on my door and, from the misty air outside through the steam rising into my face from the plate of hot food and steaming cup of coffee I'm carrying, come figures wrapped in coats and scarves, carrying bags and bundles, one holding out in two hands a baking tray full of a large beautifully cooked bird, another with boxes. 'We've brought the decorations,' the youngest one says, peering round a teddy she is heaving, as big as herself. 'We made them at home. You don't have to do anything. Happy Christmas.'

Happy Christmas! Happy Christmas! Voices echoed from the doorway, down the street and out into the night beyond, mine with them, but the mist and the damp and the dark were swirling into the house so I had to shut the door and see to the fire and welcome in my happy Christmas.

114

The Lists

Note to the Lists

Plants do not grow according to our clock-time, and our months are for regulating our activities not theirs. Length of light dominates most plants' growth, although temperature is involved in the opening of flowers and affects scent.

What plants do, and when, varies according to the soil, the plant's strength, rainfall at certain stages, its position in a garden, possibly what happened to it the previous year, even what is growing nearby. We all know that some parts of the country will be 'a month ahead' of others, and that in the same area bees will be drawn to purple cascades of aubrieta on a sunny wall in the valley when there is nothing doing up on the hill. Even in the same garden in the same year there can be variations, let alone from year to unreliable year. A sheltered backyard in London might see its first daffodil breaking while the drifts in the parks are still green in the bud. These can be weeks ahead of where I live, which is on the last high outcrop before the southern Cotswolds fall away to the Bristol plain to the south-west.

Circumstances which have nothing to do with a plant have to be taken into account when considering when, and whether, it smells. The subjectivity, and perhaps thence the elusiveness, of the effects of smell, is a main factor. Not only does olfactory functioning vary greatly between nose and nose, but equipment excellent at times may be out of action at others.

Therefore these lists cannot be complete and correct in the way a dictionary aims to be. The indications in them are based on personal experience mainly in the south of England, more particularly on the south-west edge of the Cotswolds where I have lived for about twenty years. This personal experience has, of course, been enlarged by information from better gardeners and more sensitive noses, and that again checked with books, nurseries and seed packets. Books and written instructions inevitably present a sort of abstract, an average taken from many diverse particulars.

I have not included hothouse or indoor plants which many people grow for their fragrance. Smells are carried on the air, so it is really what grows outside, commingling with all the other wafts on the airwaves, that contribute. I have included, however, plants which we may have to start off inside, and bring in again for the winter. It will be for you, living in your own place with its individual seasons, to decide, or rather to register, when 'winter' begins. If you are in my position, you will merely follow what happens through the months, sometimes able to note it, determined to use your observations in time for next year. When 'next year' turns out somewhat other than planned, when your imaginative ordering is disturbed by having to get on with living your life, comfort yourself that the life of the garden, and the air beyond, undirected by you, will provide you with serendipity enough.

List 1: Plants and when they smell

Nearly all plants and living matter smell of something to some noses, even if it's only what we think of as green and fresh. I have included in this list plants I have not had a smell from, but which others have, and plants where there are one or two varieties mentioned in books as fragrant in a generally non-scent-giving species (eg camellias). There well may be plants you get a smell from which I have not listed. I hope so. The context of a plant matters more with smell than with the other senses.

How we receive scents and how they affect us is still one of the lesser known aspects of how the brain works, but how scent is produced by plants is something chemists, perfumiers and now aromatherapists have detailed knowledge of. Roots, bark, leaf, flower and fruit can all produce scent but will do so in different ways. It is a chemical process. The sense of smell, together with taste, is referred to as the 'chemical sense'.

The main division is between scent released from leaves by contact as the scent carriers are on the surface, and from flowers which depend on temperature to produce and release the substance that sends scent on to the air. In addition, day-smelling flowers need light, and night-smelling ones lack of it.

I have given a flowering period for plants even when the chief odour does not come from the flower. These can only be approximate, the conditions for flowering being so complex and variable. With those whose leaves are aromatic, or where we are going to use the root, bulb, stem or leaf, removing the flower will prolong and strengthen those parts. Dead-heading flowers will prolong the flowering period, or encourage a separate, later period. On the other hand, you might want to leave the dying flowers for the seed.

In this List, the plants are listed alphabetically by a common English name. Where no separate English name from the Latin is commonly used, the anglicisation of the Latin is given. The Latin classificatory name is then given in italic (eg acidanthera *Acidanthera*). The sub-entries are listed in italic in their Latin form with the English or anglicised Latin name in brackets afterwards.

There are a few exceptions to this: where a plant is rarely referred to by its Latin name, then the information is given under the common name, with the Latin name referred back to the common name (eg alyssum *Lobularia*). Vegetables appear under their common name only.

There may be some marvellous-smelling plant that is your chief olfactory joy of the year, which you do not find here. You may have certain flowers blooming at times other than the months given here. The entries in the List can only be a selection from the cornucopia of plant life that will burgeon in your patch if you will let it. In condensing living matter into a written order, you have to accept that the growing habits of plants, and the olfactory reactions of individuals, won't restrict themselves to our rigid categories.

key: fl flower; lf leaf; fr fruit.

acacia, false (robinia *qv*) *Robinia*		
acidanthera (gladiolus *qv*) *Gladiolus*		
aesculus (horse chestnut *qv*) *Aesculus*		
agastache (anise *qv*) *Agastache*		
agrimony *Agrimonia eupatoria*	fl	August–September
alecost (tanacetum *qv*) *Tanacetum*		
allium *Allium*		
A. *moly* (golden garlic)	bulb	always
	lf	March–July
	fl	June–July
(chive, garlic, leek, onion, shallot *qv*)		
almond (prunus *qv*) *Prunus*		
aloysia *Aloysia triphylla* syn *Lippia*		
citriodora (lemon verbena)	lf	April–September
	fl	August
alyssum *Lobularia maritima*	fl	May–November
anethum (dill *qv*) *Anethum*		
angelica *Angelica archangelica*	whole	
	plant	March–September
	fl	May–July
anise *Agastache foeniculum*	lf	May–August
	fl	July–August
	seed	August
anthriscus *Anthriscus*		
A. *cerefolium* (chervil *qv*)		
A. *sylvestris* (cow parsley *qv*)		
antirrhinum (snapdragon) *Antirrhinum*		
majus	fl	July–October
aponogeton *Aponogeton distachyos*		
(water hawthorn)	fl	June–October

apple *Malus* many species	fl	May–June
	fr	August–November
M. sylvestris (crab apple)	fl	May–June
	fr	August–November
armorica (horseradish *qv*) *Armorica*		
artemisia *Artemisia*	lf	most months
A. abrotanum (southernwood)	fl	July–August
A. absinthium (wormwood)	fl	July–September
A. dracunculus (tarragon *qv*)		
A. lactiflora (white mugwort)	fl	August–September
A. stelleriana (beach wormwood)	fl	August–September
asperula (woodruff *qv*) *Galium*		
aster *Aster* large group		
A. novae-angliae	fl	September–October
A. novi-belgii (Michaelmas daisy)	fl	September–October
astrantia *Astrantia major*	fl	June–September
auricula (primula *qv*) *Primula*		
autumn crocus (colichicum *qv*) *Colichicum*		
azalea *Rhododendron*		
R. 'Corneille'	fl	May–June
R. Ghent hybrids	fl	May–June
R. 'Gloria Mundi'	fl	May
R. luteum (honeysuckle azalea)	fl	May
R. 'Narcissiflorum'	fl	May–June
R. occidentale	fl	June–July
barberry (berberis *qv*) *Berberis*		
basil *Ocimum basilicum*	lf	June–September
	fl	August
bay, sweet (laurus *qv*) *Laurus*		

bean: broad	lf	March–June
	fl	May–August
	pod	June–September
French	fl	June–September
	pod	July–September
runner	fl	July–September
	pod	August–September
berberis (barberry) Berberis large group		
B. buxifolia	fl	March–April
B. sargentiana	fl	April–May
bergamot (monarda qv) Monarda		
blackberry	fl	June–August
	fr	July–October
blackcurrant see currant		
bluebell Hyacinthoides non-scriptus	fl	April
borage Borago officinalis	lf	April–October
	fl	May–August
box (buxus qv) Buxus		
bracken Pteridium	lf	March–November
broom Cytisus and Genista		
C. battandieri (pineapple broom)	fl	June–July
G. aetnensis (Mount Etna broom)	fl	July–August
G. cinera	fl	May–June
buddleia Buddleia		
B. davidii 'Peace'	fl	July–October
burnet Sanguisorba officinalis	lf	March–October
	fl	May–September
buxus (box) Buxus		
B. microphylla	lf	always
B. sempervirens	lf	always
	fl	July–August

calendula (marigold) *Calendula*		
officinalis (pot marigold)	lf	always
	fl	most months
callistephus (China aster) *Callistephus*	fl	July–October
calycanthus *Calycanthus floridus*		
(Carolina allspice)	lf	April–September
	fl	May–June
camellia *Camellia sasanqua*	fl	October–March
candytuft (iberis *qv*) *Iberis*		
caraway *Carum carvi*	lf	April–October
	fl	July–August
	seed	September–November
carnation *Dianthus*		
D. 'Bookham Perfume'	fl	June
D. caryophyllus	fl	July
carrot	lf	April–November
	root	July–November
carum (caraway *qv*) *Carum*		
catmint (nepeta *qv*) *Nepeta*		
celeriac	whole plant	May–November
celery	whole plant	May–November
centaurea (knapweed) *Centaurea*		
C. cyanus (cornflower)	fl	July–September
C. moschata (sweet sultan)	fl	June–September
cestrum *Cestrum parqui* (willow-leaved		
jessamine)	fl	July–September
chaenomeles (flowering quince) *Chaenomeles*		
C. japonica (japonica, Japanese	fl	January–April
quince)	fr	June–November

124

chamomile *Chamaemelum*
  C. nobile syn *Anthemis nobilis*
    (lawn chamomile)   fl   June–August
cheiranthus (wallflower *qv*) *Erysimum*
cherry (prunus *qv*) *Prunus*
cherry pie (heliotrope *qv*) *Heliotropum*
chervil *Anthriscus cerefolium*   lf   June–October
chimonanthus (wintersweet)
  Chimonanthus praecox   fl   December–March
China aster (callistephus *qv*) *Callistephus*
chive   lf   March–September
                                       fl   May–July
choisya *Choisya ternata* (Mexican
  orange blossom)   lf   always
                                       fl   April–May
Christmas rose (hellebore *qv*) *Helleborus*
chrysanthemum *Chrysanthemum*
  large group   lf   April–November
                                       fl   July–November
cistus (rock rose) *Cistus*   lf   always
  C. x *aguilarii*   fl   June–July
  C. x *cyprius*   fl   June–July
  C. ladanifer (gum cistus)   lf   always
                                       fl   June
clary *Salvia sclarea*   lf   April
                                       fl   August
clematis *clematis* large group
  C. armandii   fl   April
  C. heracleifolia   fl   June–July
  C. montana   fl   May
  C. recta   fl   June–July

C. rehderiana	fl	August
C. vitalba (traveller's joy *qv*)		
clerodendrum *Clerodendrum*		
trichotomum	lf	May–September
	fl	July–September
clover *Trifolium*	fl	June–September
colchicum (autumn crocus) *Colchicum*		
C. autumnale meadow saffron	fl	September–October
C. speciosum	fl	September–October
comfrey *Symphytum officinale*	lf &	
	stem	April–October
	fl	June–September
convallaria (lily-of-the-valley)		
Convallaria	fl	May
coriander *Coriandrum sativum*	lf	May–October
	fl	July–September
	seed	October
cornflower (centaurea *qv*) *Centaurea*		
coronilla *Coronilla valentina*	fl	April–May
corydalis *Corydalis lutea*	fl	May–September
corylopsis *Corylopsis*	fl	March–April
cotinus (smoke bush) *Cotinus*		
coggyria syn *Rhus cotinus* f.		
purpureus	lf	April–October
	fl	July
cotoneaster *Cotoneaster* large group	fl	May–June
cotton lavender (santolina *qv*) *Santolina*		
cow parsley *Anthriscus sylvestris*	fl	May–June
cowslip *Primula veris*	fl	March–May
crab apple (malus *qv*) *Malus*		
cranesbill (geranium *qv*) *Geranium*		

crataegus (hawthorn *qv*) *Crataegus*
crinum *Crinum*

C. asiaticum	fl	July
C. powellii	fl	July–September

crocus *Crocus* large group

C. ancyrensis 'Golden Bunch'	fl	February–March
C. angustifolia syn *susianus*		
'Cloth of Gold'	fl	February
C. aureus syn *C. flavus*	fl	February
C. chrysanthus	fl	February
C. imperati	fl	December–February
C. laevigatus	fl	October–December
C. sativus (saffron crocus)	fl	October
C. speciosus	fl	October

currant *Ribes*

	stem	always
black	lf	March–October
	fl	May
	fr	July
red	fl	May
	fr	July
R. sanguineum (flowering currant)	fl	March–May

cyclamen *Cyclamen persicum*   fl   March–April
cydonia (common quince) *Cydonia*

oblonga	fl	May
	fr	September–November

cytisus (broom *qv*) *Cytisus*

daffodil (narcissus *qv*) *Narcissus*
dahlia *Dahlia* many hybrids from

D. coccinea, D. pinnata, D. rosea	fl	July–October

daisy bush (oleria *qv*) *Olearia*

dandelion *Taraxacum officinale*	lf	always
	root	always
	fl	March–June
daphne *Daphne*		
D. *bholua*	fl	January–February
D. *blagayana*	fl	March–April
D. x *burkwoodii*	fl	April–May
D. *cneorum*	fl	May–June
D. *laureola* (spurge laurel)	fl	February–March
D. *mezereum*	fl	February–March
D. *odora*	fl	January–March
day lily (hemerocallis *qv*) *Hemerocallis*		
dead nettle (lamium *qv*) *Lamium*		
deutzia *Deutzia*		
D. *compacta*	fl	May–June
D. x *elegantissima*	fl	May–June
dianthus *Dianthus* large group which includes carnation *qv*), pink (*qv*) and sweet william (*qv*)		
dictamnus *Dictamnus alba* (burning bush)	fl	June–July
digitalis (foxglove *qv*) *Digitalis*		
dill *Anethum graveolens*	lf	April–September
	fl	June–August
	seed	August–September
elder, black *Sambucus nigra*	stem	always
	lf	April–September
	fl	May–June
	fr	August–September

erica (heather) *Erica*

E. *arborea* (tree heath)	fl	March
E. *carnea* (winter heath)	fl	December–March
E. *ciliaris* (Dorset heath)	fl	July–November
E. *cinerea* (bell heather)	fl	June–October
E. *lusitanica* (Portuguese heath)	fl	January–May

erysimum (wallflower *qv*) *Erysimum*

eucalyptus (gum tree) *Eucalyptus*	stem	always
E. *gunnii* syn *divaricata*	lf	always
	fl	July–August

evening primrose (oenothera *qv*)
 Oenothera

fennel *Foeniculum vulgare*	lf	March–October
	fl	July–August
	seed	September–October

feverfew (tanacetum *qv*) *Tanacetum*
filipendula (meadowsweet *qv*)
 Filipendula
flowering currant (ribes *qv*) *Ribes*
foeniculum (fennel *qv*) *Foeniculum*
forget-me-not (myosotis *qv*) *Myosotis*

foxglove *Digitalis*	fl	June

freesia *Freesia*

F. *alba*	fl	February–March
F. 'Everett'	fl	February–March
F. 'Rijnveld's Yellow'	fl	February–March
F. 'White Swan'	fl	February–March

fritillary *Fritillaria*

F. *imperialis*	fl	April–May
F. *meleagris* (snake's-head)	fl	May

galanthus (snowdrop) *Galanthus*		
G. *allenii*	fl	February–March
G. *nivalis*	fl	January–March
galium (woodruff, sweet *qv*) *Galium*		
garlic	bulb	always
	fl	June
genista (broom *qv*) *Genista*		
geranium (cranesbill) *Geranium* large		
group	lf	always
	fl	June–August
G. *dalmaticum*	fl	June–August
G. *macrorrhizum*	fl	May–July
G. *pretense* (meadow cranesbill)	fl	May–October
G. *robertianum* (herb robert *qv*)		
germander (teucrium *qv*) *Teucrium*		
gladiolus *Gladiolus callianthus* syn		
Acidanthera bicolor var *murielaie*	fl	September–October
golden rod *Solidago*	fl	August–September
gooseberry *Ribes uva-crispa*	fl	April–May
	fr	July
gorse *Ulex*		
U. *europaeus* (furze, whin)	fl	almost always
U. *gallii* (dwarf gorse)	fl	almost always
grape hyacinth (muscari *qv*) *Muscari*		
grass	lf	always
guelder rose (viburnum *qv*) *Vibernum*		
gum tree (eucalyptus *qv*) *Eucalyptus*		
hamamelis (witch hazel) *Hamamelis*	bark	always
H. *japonica* (Japanese witch hazel)	fl	February–March
H. *j.* 'Zuccariniana'	fl	March–April
H. *mollis* (Chinese witch hazel)	fl	December–March

hawthorn *Crataegus monogyna*	fl	May
heather (erica *qv*) *Erica*		
hebe *Hebe*		
H. *cupressoides*	fl	June
hedera (ivy) *Hedera*	fl	September–November
helianthus (sunflower) *Helianthus*		
annuus	fl	July–September
heliotrope *Heliotropum arborescens*		
(cherry pie)	fl	May–October
hellebore *Helleborus*		
H. *foetidus* (stinking hellebore)	fl	March–May
H. *niger* (Christmas rose)	fl	December–March
H. *orientalis* (Lenten rose)	fl	February–March
hemerocallis (day lily) *Hemerocallis*		
H. *citrina*	fl	July–August
H. *dumortieri*	fl	May
H. *lilioasphodelus* syn H. *flava*	fl	April–May
herb robert *Geranium robertianum*	lf	always
	fl	June–November
hesperis *Hesperis matronalis* (sweet		
rocket)	fl	June
honesty (lunaria *qv*) *Lunaria*	fl	
honeysuckle (lonicera *qv*) *Lonicera*		
hop *Humulus lupulus*	fl	August–September
horehound *Marrubium vulgare*		
(white horehound)	lf	April–September
	fl	June–July
horse chestnut *Aesculus*	fl	May–June
horseradish *Armorica rusticana*	lf	June–September
	root	always
humulus (hop *qv*) *Humulus*		
hyacinth *Hyacinthus*	fl	March–May

131

hyacinthoides (bluebell *qv*) *Hyacinthoides*
hypericum (St John's wort) *Hypericum*

H. balearicum	fl	May–September
H. calycinum (Rose of Sharon)	fl	June–September
hyssop *Hyssopus officinalis*	lf	always
	fl	July–September

iberis (candytuft) *Iberis*

I. amara	fl	June–September
I. odorata	fl	June–September
I. umbellata	fl	May–June
ionopsidium *Ionopsidium acaule*		
(violet cress)	fl	June–September

iris *Iris* large group

I. danfordiae	fl	January–February
I. florentina (orris root)	fl	May–June
I. germanica	fl	May–June
I. graminea	fl	June
I. histrioides	fl	January–February
I. pallida	fl	May
I. reticulata	fl	February–March
I. unguicularis syn *I. stylosa*	fl	November–March
itea *Itea ilicifolia*	fl	August

ivy (hedera *qv*) *Hedera*

japonica (chaenomeles *qv*) *Chaenomeles*
 japonica
jasmine *Jasminum*

J. officinale	fl	June–September
J. stephanense	fl	June

Jerusalem artichoke	root	November–February
jonquil (narcissus *qv*) *Narcissus*		
juniper *Juniperus* large group	lf	always
	stem	always
knapweed (centaurea *qv*) *Centaurea*		
laburnum *Laburnum*	fl	May–June
lamium (dead nettle) *Lamium*	fl	May–July
lathyrus *Lathyrus*		
L. odorata (sweet pea)	fl	June–September
L. sylvestris (perpetual)	fl	July
laurelia (laurel) *Laurelia sempervirens*		
syn *L. serrata*	fl	May
laurus *Laurus nobilis* (sweet bay)	lf	always
lavender *Lavandula*	stem	always
	lf	March–November
	fl	June–August
leek	whole	
	plant	June–February
lemon balm *Melissa officinalis*	lf	April–October
	fl	June–August
lemon verbena (aloysia *qv*) *Aloysia*		
Lenten rose (hellebore *qv*) *Helleborus*		
leucojum (snowflake) *Leucojum*		
L. autumnale	fl	July–September
L. vernum	fl	February–March
levisticum (lovage *qv*) *Levisticum*		
ligustrum (privet) *Ligustrum vulgare*	fl	May–July
lilac (syringa *qv*) *Syringa*		

lily *Lilium*
L. *auratum*	fl	August–September
L. *candidum* (Madonna)	fl	June–July
L. *longiflorum* (Easter)	fl	July–August
L. *martagon* (Turkscap)	fl	June–July
L. *regale*	fl	July
L. *speciosum*	fl	August–September

lily-of-the-valley (convallaria *qv*) *Convallaria*

lime *Tilia*	fl	July

limnanthes (poached egg plant)
Limnanthes douglasii	fl	June–August

lobularia (alyssum *qv*) *Lobularia*

lonicera (honeysuckle) *Lonicera*
L. *americana*	fl	April–June
L. *fragrantissima*	fl	December–February
L. *japonica* 'Halliana'	fl	July–September
L. *nitida*	fl	May

L. *periclymenum* (woodbine)
L. *p.* 'Belgica'	fl	May–June
L. *p.* 'Serotina'	fl	July–October
L. x *purpusii*	fl	December–February
lovage *Levisticum officinale*	lf	April–September
	fl	July–August
lunaria (honesty) *Lunaria*	fl	April–June
lupin *Lupinus*	fl	May–June
L. *arboreus* (tree lupin)	fl	May

magnolia *Magnolia*
M. *grandiflora*	fl	June–August
M. *kobus*	fl	March–April
M. *sieboldii*	fl	May

M. x *soulangeana*	fl	March–April
M. stellata	fl	March–April
M. wilsonii	fl	May
mahonia *Mahonia japonica*	fl	January–March
malcolmia *Malcolmia maritima*		
(Virginian stock)	fl	May–September
marigold (calendula *qv*) *Calendula*		
marjoram (oregano) *Origanum*	lf	always
	fl	July–August
marrubium (horehound *qv*) *Marrubium*		
marvel of Peru (mirabilis *qv*) *Mirabilis*		
matthiola (stock) *Matthiola*		
M. bicornis (night-scented)	fl	June–October
M. Brompton	fl	May–June
M. Ten Week	fl	June–August
meadowsweet *Filipendula ulmaria*		
syn *Spiraea ulmaria*	fl	May–June
meconopsis *Meconopsis cambrica*		
(Welsh poppy)	fl	June–September
melissa (lemon balm *qv*) *Melissa*		
mentha (mint *qv*) *Mentha*		
Mexican orange blossom (choisya *qv*) *Choisya*		
michaelmas daisy (aster *qv*) *Aster*		
mignonette (reseda *qv*) *Reseda*		
mint *Mentha*		
M. aquatica (water mint)	lf	April–October
	fl	July–September
M. x *piperita* f *citrata* (lemon mint)	lf	April–October
	fl	July–September
M. pulegium (pennyroyal)	lf	April–October
	fl	July–September

M. spicata (spearmint)	lf	April–October
	fl	July–September
M. suaveolens syn *M. rotundifolia*		
(apple mint)	lf	April–October
	fl	July–September
mirabilis (marvel of Peru)		
Mirabilis	fl	July
mock orange (philadelphus *qv*) *Philadelphus*		
monarda (bergamot) *Monarda*	lf	April–October
M. didyma	fl	June–September
M. fistulosa (wild bergamot)	fl	June–August
muscari (grape hyacinth) *Muscari*		
M. armeniacum	fl	April–May
M. neglectum syn *M. racemosum*	fl	April–May
myosotis (forget-me-not) *Myosotis*	fl	April–June
myrrhis (sweet cicely) *Myrrhis*		
odorata	lf	April–September
	fl	June
narcissus (daffodil, jonquil) *Narcissus*	fl	February–June
large group of which the Trumpet		
Narcissi are known as daffodils	fl	February–April
N. cyclamineus	fl	February–March
N. jonquilla (wild jonquil)	fl	March–April
N.j. 'Bobbysoxer'	fl	April
N. papyraceus syn *N.* 'Paper White'	fl	March–April
N. poeticus	fl	April
var. *recurvus* (old pheasant's eye)	fl	May
N. pseudonarcissus (wild daffodil)	fl	March–April
N. tazetta	fl	January–February
nasturtium (tropaeolum *qv*) *Tropaeolum*		

nepeta (catmint) *Nepeta*		
N. cataria	lf	April–October
	fl	June–September
N. x *faassenii*	lf	April–November
	fl	May–September
nettle *Urtica dioica*	lf	February–December
	fl	May–September
nicotiana (tobacco plant) *Nicotiana*	fl	July–September
ocimum (basil qv) *Ocimum basilicum*		
oenothera (evening primrose)		
Oenothera	fl	June–September
olearia (daisy bush) *Olearia*		
O. x *haastii*	fl	July–August
O. ilicifolia (mountain holly)	fl	June
	lf	always
O. x *mollis*	fl	May
onion	bulb	always
	lf	March–September
	fl	June–July
origano (marjoram *qv*) *Origanum*		
osmanthus *Osmanthus*		
O. x *burkwoodii*	fl	April–May
O. delavayi	fl	April
O. fragrans (fragrant olive)	fl	May–August
paeonia (peony) *Paeonia*		
P. 'Albert Crousse'	fl	June
P. lactifolia (Chinese)	fl	June
P. officinalis	fl	May

pancratium (sea lily) *Pancratium*	fl	July–September
P. maritimum (sea daffodil)	fl	May–June
pansy (viola *qv*) *Viola*		
parsley *Petroselinum crispum*	lf	always
	stem	always
parsnip	lf	April–January
	root	October–February
papaver (poppy *qv*) *Papaver*		
pelargonium *Pelargonium* large group		
P. capitatum (rose-scented)	lf	always
	fl	May–October
P. 'Fragrans' (pine-scented)	lf	always
	fl	May–October
P. 'Mabel Grey' (lemon-scented)	lf	always
	fl	May–October
P. 'Royal Oak' (spice-scented)	lf	always
	fl	May–October
P. tormentosum (peppermint-scented)	lf	always
	fl	May–October
pennyroyal (mentha *qv*) *Mentha*		
peony (paeonia *qv*) *Paeonia*		
petroselinum (parsley *qv*) *Petroselinum*		
petunia *Petunia*	fl	June–October
philadelphus (mock orange) *Philadelphus*		
P. 'Beauclerk'	fl	May–June
P. 'Belle Etoile'	fl	June–July
P. coronarius (mock orange)	fl	June–July
P. delavayi	fl	May–June
P. 'Lemoinei'	fl	May–June
P. microphyllus	fl	June–July

phlox *Phlox*

P. *maculata* (meadow phlox)	fl	July–September
P. *paniculata*	fl	July–September

pine *Pinus* — whole tree — always

pink *Dianthus*

D. *alpinus*	fl	May–August
D. *armeria* (Deptford pink)	fl	June–July
D. *deltoides* (maiden pink)	fl	June–October

poached egg plant (limnanthes *qv*) *Limnanthes*

polyanthus (primula *qv*) *Primula*

polygonatum (solomon's seal)

Polygonatum	fl	June

poplar *Populus* — lf — April

P. *balsamifera* (Balsam poplar)	lf	April
P. x *candicans* (Balm of Gilead)	lf	April

poppy *Papaver* large group

P. *nudicaule* (Icelandic)	fl	May–June
P. *orientale* (oriental)	fl	May–June
P. *rhoeas* (corn, Flanders)	fl	June–August
P. r. Shirley series	fl	June–August
P. *somniferum* (opium)	fl	June–September

Welsh poppy (meconopsis *qv*) *Meconopsis*

populus (poplar *qv*) *Populus*

potato: early	tuber	June–July
main	tuber	August–November
primrose *Primula vulgaris*	fl	February–April

primula *Primula* large group

P. *auricula*	fl	March–May
P. *florinda*	fl	June–July
P. *sikkimensis* (Himalayan cowslip)	fl	June–July

P. *polyantha* (polyanthus)	fl	March–April
P. *veris* (cowslip *qv*)		
P. *vulgaris* (primrose *qv*)		
privet (ligustrum *qv*) *Ligustrum*		
Prunus *Prunus* large group		
P. *dulcis* (almond)	fl	February–May
P. *conradinae* (cherry)	fl	February
P. *laurocerasus* (cherry laurel)	fl	April
P. *lusitanica* (Portugal laurel)	fl	June
P. *mume* (Japanese apricot)	fl	February
P. *spinosa* (blackthorn, sloe)	fl	March
P. x *subhirtella autumnalis*	fl	November–December
P. x *yedoensis*	fl	March–April
pyracantha *Pyracantha coccinea*		
(firethorn)	fl	June–July
quince, common (cydonia *qv*) *Cydonia*		
raspberry *Rubus idaeus*		
summer-fruiting	fl	June
	fr	July–August
autumn-fruiting	fl	August
	fr	September–October
redcurrant *see* currant		
reseda (mignonette) *Reseda odorata*	fl	June–October
rhododendron (azalea *qv*) *Rhododendron*		
rhododendron *Rhododendron*		
R. 'Angelo'	fl	June
R. *auriculatum*	fl	July–August
R. 'Beauty of Littleworth'	fl	May–June

R. cinnabarinum subsp *xanthocodon*	lf	always
	fl	May
R. discolor	fl	June–July
R. fortunei	fl	May
R. glaucophyllum	lf	always
	fl	May
R. 'Loderi'	fl	May
rhubarb *Rheum rhaponticum*	lf	March–October
	stalk	March–July
ribes (flowering currant) *Ribes*	lf	March–September
	fl	March
R. uva-crispa (gooseberry *qv*)		
robinia (false acacia) *Robinia*		
pseudoacacia	fl	May–June
rock rose (cistus *qv*) *Cistus*		
rose *Rosa* (*see* List 5)		
rosemary *Rosmarinus officinalis*	lf &	
	stem	always
	fl	March–April; September
rubus (blackberry, raspberry *qv*) *Rubus*		
rue *Ruta graveolens* (herb of grace)	lf	always
	fl	June–September
rumex (sorrel *qv*) *Rumex acetosa*		
sage *Salvia*		
S. elegans (pineapple)	lf	always
	fl	June–August
S. officinalis	lf	always
	fl	May–July
S. sclarea turkestana (clary *qv*)		

St John's wort (hypericum *qv*) *Hypericum*		
salvia (sage *qv*) *Salvia*		
sambucus (elder, black *qv*) *Sambucus*		
sanguisorba (burnet *qv*) *Sanguisorba*		
santolina (cotton lavender) *Santolina*	lf	always
saponaria (soapwort) *Saponaria*	lf	April
	fl	July–August
	root	November
sarcococca *Sarcococca*	fl	January–February
satureja (winter savory *qv*) *Satureja*		
sea lily (pancratium *qv*) *Pancratium*		
shallot	bulb	always
	lf	May–September
skimmia *Skimmia japonica*	lf	always
	fl	April
sloe (prunus *qv*) *Prunus*		
smoke bush (cotinus *qv*) *Cotinus*		
snapdragon (antirrhinum *qv*) *Antirrhinum*		
snowdrop (galathus *qv*) *Galanthus*		
snowflake (leucojum *qv*) *Leucojum*		
soapwort (saponaria *qv*) *Saponaria*		
solidago (golden rod *qv*) *Solidago*		
solomon's seal (polygonatum *qv*) *Polygonatum*		
sorrel *Rumex acetosa*	lf	March–October
spinach	lf	most months
stock (matthiola *qv*) *Matthiola*		
Virginian (malcolmia *qv*) *Malcolmia*		
strawberry *Fragaria*	fl	May–July
	fr	July–August
F. vesca (wild)	fl	April–September
	fr	May–October

sunflower (helianthus *qv*) *Helianthus*
sweet cicely (myrrhis *qv*) *Myrrhis*
sweet pea (lathyrus *qv*) *Lathyrus*
sweet rocket (hesperis *qv*) *Hesperis*
sweet sultan (centaurea *qv*) *Centaurea*

sweet william *Dianthus barbatus*	fl	June–July
syringa (lilac) *Syringa*	fl	May–June
tanacetum *Tanacetum*		
T. argenteum syn *Achillea argentea*	lf	always
	fl	August
T. balsamita syn *Chrysanthemum*	lf	May–September
balsamita (alecost)	fl	June–July
T. coccineum syn *Chrysanthemum*		
coccineum (painted daisy)	lf	always
	fl	April–May
T. parthenium (feverfew)	stem	always
	lf	most months
	fl	June–November
T. vulgare (common tansy)	fl	August
taraxcum (dandelion *qv*) *Taraxcum*		
tarragon *Artemisia dracunculus*	lf	April–August
teucrium (germander) *Teucrium*		
T. fruticans (shrubby germander)	lf	always
	fl	June–September
thistle *Onopordum acanthium*	fl	July–August
thyme *Thymus*		
T. x citrodorus (lemon-scented)	lf	most months
	fl	July–September
T. herba-barona (caraway-scented)	lf	most months
	fl	July–September

T. vulgaris (common)	lf	always
	fl	June–August
tilia (lime *qv*) *Tilia*		
tobacco plant (nicotiana *qv*) *Nicotiana*		
tomato	lf &	
	stem	May–October
	fr	August–October
trachelospermum *Trachelospermum*		
asiaticum	fl	July–August
traveller's joy *Clematis vitalba*	fl	July
tropaeolum (nasturtium) *Tropaeolum*	lf	May–November
T. majus	fl	June–October
T. peregrinum syn *T. canariense*		
(canary creeper)	fl	July–November
tulip *Tulipa* large group	fl	March–June
ulex (gorse *qv*) *Ulex*		
urtica (nettle *qv*) *Urtica*		
valerian *Valeriana officinalis* (all heal)	fl	July–September
verbena *Verbena bonariensis*	fl	July–September
verbena, lemon (aloysia *qv*) *Aloysia*		
vibernum *Vibernum*		
V. x *bodnanteni* 'Dawn'	fl	December–February
V. x *b.* 'Deben'	fl	March
V. x *burkwoodii*	fl	March–May
V. x *carlcephalum*	fl	April–May
V. carlesii	fl	April–May
V. x *juddii*	fl	April–May
V. opulus (guelder rose)	fl	May–June

144

viola (pansy, violet) *Viola* large group

V. *odorata* (English violet)	fl	January–May
V. *tricolor* (heartsease)	fl	May–September
V. x *wittrockiana* (garden pansy)		
summer-flowering	fl	May–September
winter-flowering	fl	November–March

Virginian stock (malcolmia *qv*) *Malcolmia*

wallflower *Erysimum* syn *Cheiranthus*

E. *cheiri*	fl	March–May
E. *c.* 'Harpur Crewe'	fl	April–June
E. 'Moonlight'	fl	May
winter savory *Satureja montana*	lf	January–October

witch hazel (hamamelis *qv*) *Hamamelis*
wintersweet (chimonanthus *qv*) *Chimonanthus*
wistaria *Wisteria*

W. *floribunda* 'Black Dragon'	fl	May–June
W. *f.* 'Macrobotrys'	fl	May–June
W. *sinensis* 'Alba'	fl	May–June

woodruff, sweet *Galium odoratum*

syn *Asperula odorata*	fl	May–June

zenobia *Zenobia*

Z. *pulverulenta*	fl	May–June

List 2: Months and what you might be smelling in each

This list tries to give an idea of what each month might smell of. It will always be a great mixture, unlike the experience of trying to pinpoint one particular fragrance from sniffing a flower, open in the sun, or aroma from a leaf you have crushed as you walk up your garden path or on verges or tracks. Even those easily identifiable scents are often from several odoriferous substances, and may not remain the same for even a short time of sniffing.

I have not specified in this list which part of a mentioned plant may be providing that strand in the fabric of the air. January to me includes at some point the strong, refreshing irony smell of blackcurrant, the (to me) offensive smell of elder, the sweet smell of honeysuckle, the pleasing and interesting (to me) smell of parsnips.

If you don't know that a blackcurrant smell in January will be from its stem since it is deciduous (the bush coming into leaf in the spring), that it flowers in May and fruits in June and July, and it worries you not to know how a bush, whose overpowering smell you associate with a hot summer soft fruit season, can smell in the depth of winter, you can go to List 1 where you will find an indication of when stem, leaf, flower and fruit may smell. Likewise, you may be surprised at honeysuckle so early in the year. You may be aware that there are honeysuckles for each season. You would like to have that heavenly scent when little else seems to you delightful in your garden and you want to know which honeysuckle to get. You can look under honeysuckle in List 1 where you will find its Latin name *Lonicera*. Under *Lonicera* in that List, and also in encyclopaedias of gardening and botanical books and nurserymen's catalogues, you will find the horticultural information you are seeking. (In my List 1 *L. fragrantissima* and *L.* x *purpusii* are down as flowering from

December to February.) Of course, the composition of the airwaves contains a great deal we can never trace back to a particular plant on a horticultural list, so you will not find every whiff you get from this list, or indeed from your own experience of the changing air through the months of the year, explained in a horticultural list or even List 1 in this book.

I hope, however, that some of you, who may not have a garden and don't want to bother with horticultural details, will enjoy this list just as an echo (or the odoriferous equivalent of what an echo is to sound – a memory? an olfactory illusion?) of the experience of taking in the scent-laden air as it gradually and subtly changes its composition through the unfolding year.

January
blackcurrant, box, Christmas rose, crocus, daphne, elder, feverfew, gorse, grass, heather, herb robert, honeysuckle, iris, Jerusalem artichoke, juniper, leek, mahonia, marigold, parsley, parsnip, rosemary, sarcococca, snowdrop, thyme, winter savory, wintersweet, witch hazel (Chinese)

February
blackcurrant, box, bean (broad), cotton lavender, crocus, daffodil, daphne, elder, feverfew, gorse, grass, heather, herb robert, honeysuckle, iris, juniper, lavender, Lenten rose, mahonia, marigold, parsley, parsnip, primrose, potatoes (seed), rosemary, sarcococca, shallot, snowdrop, violet, wintersweet, witch hazel (Chinese)

March
almond, auricula, blackcurrant, box, crocus, daffodil, daphne, elder, feverfew, garlic (golden), gorse, grass, hellebore (stinking), iris, jonquil, lavender, magnolia, mahonia, marigold, onion, primrose, rosemary, shallot, viola, violet, winter savory

April

almond, bay, berberis, blackcurrant, box, carrot, chrysanthemum, cotton lavender, crocus, daffodil, daphne, feverfew, fritillary, garlic (golden), gorse, grape hyacinth, grass, hellebore (stinking), herb robert, hyacinth, jonquil, lavender, marigold, Mexican orange blossom, onion, osmanthus, parsley, polyanthus, rosemary, skimmia, tulip, vibernum, viola, violet, wallflower

May

alecost, alyssum, apple, berberis, blackcurrant, bluebell, bean (broad), broom, carrot, catmint, cherry, chive, chrysanthemum, clematis, comfrey, cornflower, cow parsley, cowslip, cranesbill, daffodil, daphne, day lily, elder, feverfew, forget-me-not, garlic (golden), gooseberry, gorse, grape hyacinth, grass, hawthorn, herb robert, honesty, honeysuckle, horse chestnut, hop, hyacinth, iris, jonquil, juniper, laburnum, laurel, lavender, lilac, lily-of-the-valley, lupin, marigold, marjoram, Mexican orange blossom, mint, nasturtium, osmanthus, peony, pansy, pine, pink, poppy, rhubarb, rose, rue, skimmia, sweet william, spring greens, stock, strawberry, strawberry (wild), sweet cicely, tomato, tulip, vibernum, wistaria, wallflower

June

alecost, alyssum, apple, astrantia, azalea, berberis, bean (broad, French), bergamot, blackberry, blackcurrant, borage, broom, buddleia, carnation, carrot, catmint, chamomile, chive, clematis, clover, comfrey, cornflower, cranesbill, day lily, dill, elder, evening primrose, foxglove, garlic (golden), geranium, gooseberry, gorse, grass, herb robert, honeysuckle, hop, horse chestnut, iris, jasmine, lavender, leek, lemon balm, lilac, lily, lupin, marigold, marjoram, meadowsweet, mignonette, mint, mock orange, nasturtium, pansy, peony, pink, poppy, primula, privet, rue, St John's wort, salvia, stock, strawberry, strawberry (wild), sweet pea, sweet rocket, sweet william, thyme, tomato, tulip, wallflower, wistaria, zenobia

July

alecost, alyssum, angelica, artemisia (southernwood), aster, basil, bergamot, bean (broad, French, runner), blackcurrant, borage, bracken, broom, candytuft, carnation, carrot, celery, chamomile, chive, chrysanthemum, clematis, comfrey, cornflower, cotton lavender, cranesbill, dahlia, dead nettle, dill, elder, evening primrose, fennel, feverfew, garlic (golden), gooseberry, gorse, grass, heather, herb robert, honeysuckle, iris, jasmine, juniper, lavender, leek, lemon balm, lily, lime, lovage, marigold, meadowsweet, mignonette, mint, mock orange, nasturtium, phlox, pink, poppy, potato, primula, privet, raspberry, redcurrant, rosemary, rue, sage, sea lily, shallot, strawberry, strawberry (wild), sunflower, sweet pea, sweet rocket, thistle, thyme, tomato, trachelospermum, traveller's joy, verbena, winter savory, zenobia

August

acidanthera, alecost, alyssum, angelica, apple, artemisia (southernwood), aster, basil, bean (broad, French, runner), bergamot, blackberry, blackcurrant, borage, bracken, broom, buddleia, carnation, carrot, catmint, chamomile, chive, chrysanthemum, clematis, comfrey, cornflower, cranesbill, crocus, day lily, dill, elder, evening primrose, fennel, feverfew, geranium, golden rod, gorse, grass, heather, herb robert, honeysuckle, hop, horseradish, itea, japonica, jasmine, lavender, leek, lemon balm, lemon verbena, lily, lovage, marjoram, marigold, mignonette, mint, nasturtium, onion, pansy, phlox, pine, pink, polyanthus, poppy, potato, privet, rue, sage, sea lily, snapdragon, stock, strawberry (wild), sweet pea, sweet rocket, sweet sultan, thistle, thyme, tobacco plant, tomato, trachelospermum, verbena, winter savory

September

acidanthera, alecost, alyssum, apple, artemisia (wormwood), aster, autumn crocus, basil, bay, bean (broad, French, runner), bergamot, blackberry, blackcurrant, borage, box, bracken, catmint, China aster, chive, chrysanthemum, clematis, clerodendrum, clover; comfrey, cornflower, cranesbill, carnation, dill, elder, eucalyptus, evening primrose, fennel, feverfew, gorse, grass, heather, herb robert, honeysuckle, hop, horehound, horseradish, hyssop, ivy, japonica, jasmine, lavender, lemon balm, lemon verbena, lovage, marigold, marjoram, Michaelmas daisy, mint, nasturtium, nettle, onion, pansy, parsely, parsnip, pennyroyal, phlox, pink, poppy, potato, privet, quince (common), rosemary, rue, sage, sea lily, spinach, stock, strawberry (wild), sunflower, sweet cicely, sweet pea, sweet sultan, thyme, tobacco plant, tomato, verbena, Virginian stock, winter savory

October

alyssum, apple, aster, autumn crocus, bay, bean (French, runner), blackberry, bracken, buddleia, carrot, chive, chrysanthemum, comfrey, cornflower, cotton lavender, cranesbill, dandelion, feverfew, gorse, heather, herb robert, honeysuckle, japonica, lavender, leek, lemon balm, marigold, Michaelmas daisy, mignonette, Michaelmas daisy, nasturtium, parsley, pink, potato, quince (common), sage, spinach, stock, strawberry (wild), sweet pea, thyme, tobacco plant, tomato, verbena, winter savory

November

alyssum, apple, autumn crocus, blackcurrant, bracken, camellia, carrot, chrysanthemum, cranesbill, dandelion, elder, eucalyptus, evening primrose, feverfew, gorse, grass, heather, ivy, japonica, lavender, leek, marigold, marjoram, nasturtium, parsley, parsnip, potato, quince (common), rosemary, sage, sorrel, spinach, thyme, verbena

December

blackcurrant, box, Christmas rose, cotton lavender, cranesbill, dandelion, elder, eucalyptus, feverfew, gorse, grass, heather, herb robert, honeysuckle, horseradish, hyssop, iris, juniper, lavender, leek, marigold, marjoram, parsley, parsnip, rosemary, sage, sorrel, spinach, thyme, wintersweet

Note to Lists 3 and 4:
Plants and what to do when & Months and what you might be doing in each

For these lists of possible action I have given the simplest of suggestions. They should not be taken as instructions, but more as reminders of when you need to be thinking of and preparing for certain activities in relation to the particular plants you want to grow.

If you think you would like to have something out in January or in October, then, armed with a name, you can go to some of the many excellent manuals to find detailed advice. If there is by chance a fine day at the end of February, and you have some time and strength, then it is better to see what you could be doing in order to enjoy sweet peas in July than wishing – as you gaze at your neighbour's garden bright with early daffodils – that you had planted bulbs in September.

When you sow what, will depend to some extent on the climate where you live. Most seed won't germinate until the earth is warm enough for that particular genus. Some seed is sown inside, and the seedlings that emerge planted out in pots or trays to give them room to grow, but kept sheltered until they are strong enough, and the weather clement enough, to be planted outside. The magic phrase is 'after fear of frost has passed'. (Of course, frost doesn't always keep away just because we have stopped fearing it.) This is also the time you can put out half-hardy plants you have brought in for the winter; for instance, geraniums.

Other seed is sown straight into the ground. There are some plants which do perfectly well sown direct into the ground in, say, May. They can be given an early start by sowing them inside in February–April and then planting them out outside later. China asters, leeks, marrows are examples. It is not only bad weather one is trying to get the better of by this, but all the things that are looking for fresh green meals early in the year from the soil just as much as we want the seedlings to grow into dinner for us later. A second sowing outside can then be made so you will have a succession of flowers and produce and don't have to eat thirty lettuces in one week.

For annuals (and we treat most vegetables as annuals), there is generally a period over several weeks in which you can sow. Seed packets usually give the information needed and you can supplement that information with one of the practical manuals available. Better still, ask someone with a garden you like near to yours for advice.

Once again I would stress that the calendar time which we live by, and which I have given in these lists, is only a very rough approximation to plant time and weather time. The indication 'April–June' or 'November–March' for an action means that at some time during that period when the weather, soil and your own circumstances are right for it, you can sow or plant; not that you will be doing it in each month covered.

In this list, where I have not specified 'inside', 'sow' means outside, direct into the ground. 'Planting out' and 'planting outside' are not the same. In an attempt to keep my suggestions simple I have not gone into all the intermediary stages and terms. These you will find explained in the practical manuals.

153

List 3: Plants and what to do when

acidanthera	plant corm in March
alecost	root division in spring or autumn
allium	plant/divide bulbs in autumn
almond	plant November–March
alyssum	sow inside February–March, plant outside May–June; sow outside April–May
angelica	sow in early autumn
antirrhinum	sow inside January–February; plant out in May
apple	plant November–March
artemisia	plant in October or March
artichoke (Jerusalem)	plant in February
aster (perennial)	plant in autumn or spring
China aster (annual)	sow inside in March, plant out May–June; sow outside April–May
auricula	sow inside March–April, plant out May–June, transplant in autumn; divide after flowering
azalea	plant October–March
basil	sow indoors in March, plant out in June; sow outdoors in May
bay	plant March or September
bean (broad)	sow in November or February–April
(French)	sow inside in March, plant out in May; sow outside April–June
(runner)	sow inside in March, plant out end May–June; sow outside May–June
berberis	plant in autumn or late winter
bergamot	plant in autumn or spring
blackcurrant	plant autumn–spring
borage	sow in April

box	plant in September–October
broom	plant autumn–spring
buddleia	plant autumn–spring
burnet	sow in April. Self-seeding
camellia	plant spring–summer
candytuft	sow March–April
caraway	(biennial) sow in September, transplant in spring
carnation	plant in autumn or spring
carrot	(early varieties) sow March–June; (maincrop) sow April–July
catmint	plant autumn–spring
celeriac	sow inside in March, plant out in May
celery	sow inside in March, plant out May–June
chamomile	sow in spring or autumn; plant/divide in autumn or spring
cherry	plant autumn–spring
cherry laurel	plant autumn–spring
cherry pie	plant in June. Lift and pot inside before frost
chive	plant/divide in March
Christmas rose	plant spring or autumn
chrysanthemum	(annual) sow March–April or September; (hardy perennial) plant autumn–spring; (border) cuttings of stools inside January–March, plant out in May. Lift plants for stock in October
clary	sow in April
clematis	plant in March or October
clerodendrum	plant autumn–spring
comfrey	plant autumn–spring
coriander	sow in April

cornflower	(annual) sow in April; (perennial) plant/divide autumn or spring
corylopsis	sow in autumn
cotoneaster	plant autumn–spring
cowslip	sow inside March–April, plant out May–June; divide after flowering
crab apple	plant autumn–spring
cranesbill	plant/divide in spring or autumn
crocus	(spring-flowering) plant in early autumn; (autumn-flowering) plant July–August
daffodil	plant late summer–winter
dahlia	start stored or bought tubers into growth inside in February, and when shoots are strong enough, take cuttings or divide tubers. Plant out May–June. Lift tubers in late autumn when top growth is blackened by frost
daisy bush	plant in autumn or spring
daphne	plant autumn–spring
day lily	plant March–April or in October
dill	sow in April or September
evening primrose	(biennial) sow in April, transplant in September; (perennial) plant spring or autumn. Self-seeding
fennel	sow March–April or in August
feverfew	plant/divide in spring. Self-seeding
flowering currant	plant autumn–spring
forget-me-not	sow June–July; plant/divide in autumn. Self-seeding
foxglove	(biennal) sow in spring, transplant in autumn; (perennial) plant in spring or autumn. Self-seeding

fritillary	plant September–November
garlic	plant bulbs in November or February–March
geranium	plant in spring or autumn
gooseberry	plant autumn–spring
gorse	plant autumn–spring
grape hyacinth	plant bulb in autumn
grass	sow in April or September
guelder rose	plant autumn–spring
hawthorn	plant autumn–spring
heather	plant in April or October
honesty	sow April–May, plant August–November. Self-seeding
honeysuckle	plant autumn–spring
hop	plant in spring
horehound	sow in spring
horseradish	sow in spring; divide roots in autumn
hyacinth	plant in autumn
hyssop	plant in April; divide in autumn
ionopsidium	sow in spring or autumn
iris	(June-flowering rhizomes) plant March–April or in September; (bulbous early-flowering species) plant September–October; (fibrous-rooted species) plant in spring or autumn
itea	plant in autumn
japonica	plant autumn–spring
jasmine	plant in spring or autumn
jonquil	plant late summer–autumn
juniper	plant autumn–spring
laburnum	plant in spring or autumn
lamium	plant in spring or autumn
lavender	plant in March or September

leek	sow inside in February, sow outside in March, plant out June–July
lemon balm	sow in spring; plant out/divide in autumn. Self-seeding
lemon verbena	plant in spring or autumn; pot and bring in before frost
Lenten rose	plant in March or October–November
lilac	plant autumn–spring
lily	plant in autumn or spring
lily-of-the-valley	plant in autumn
lovage	sow in autumn; divide in March or October. Self-seeding
lupin	(annual) sow March–April; (perennial) plant in spring; (tree lupin) plant in April or October
magnolia	plant March–April or October
mahonia	sow in spring; plant autumn–spring
marigold	sow March–April or August–September. Self-seeding
marjoram	sow in spring; divide in autumn
marvel of Peru	plant in April
meadowsweet	plant autumn–spring; divide in spring
meconopsis	sow March–April
Mexican orange blossom	plant in October or March
Michaelmas daisy	plant in autumn or spring; divide and replant in spring
mignonette	sow March–April
mint	plant root in March; divide any time
mock orange	plant autumn–spring
narcissus	plant late summer–autumn
nasturtium	sow in April

onion	plant sets March–April
osmanthus	plant in April or September–October
pansy	plant April–May
parsley	sow in February, May, and August for a continuous supply
parsnip	sow in February–March
pelargonium	plant outside after danger of frost; lift and pot before frost and bring in for the winter
pennyroyal	plant in autumn or spring
peony	plant autumn–spring
petunia	sow inside February–April; plant outside late May–June
philadelphus	plant autumn–spring
poached egg plant	sow in March or September. Self-seeding
phlox	(annual) sow inside February–March, plant out in June; (herbaceous) plant/divide in spring or autumn
pink	(annual) sow inside February–March, plant out late May–June; (perennial) plant March–April or in October
poppy	(annual) sow March–April for summer flowering, in September for spring flowering; (perennial) plant March–April or in October
primrose	sow inside in March, plant out May–June; divide after flowering
privet	plant autumn–spring
prunus	plant autumn–spring
pyracantha	plant April–May or September–October
raspberry	plant canes autumn–spring
redcurrant	plant autumn–spring
rhododendron	plant autumn–spring

rhubarb	plant/divide crowns in spring or autumn
rose	plant autumn–spring
rosemary	plant autumn–spring
rue	plant in March
sage	plant autumn–spring
sarcococca	plant in spring
shallot	plant February–March
skimmia	plant autumn–spring
snowdrop	plant in autumn; transplant after flowering while still green
sorrel	sow in spring; plant/divide in autumn. Self-seeding
southernwood	plant in March or October
spinach	(summer) sow March–July; (winter) sow in August; (perpetual) sow in April. Self-seeding
stock	(annual Ten-Week) sow inside in March, plant out in May; (biennial Brompton) sow inside June–July, plant out in autumn, transplant in spring; (night-scented) sow May–July
strawberry	plant in late summer–autumn or in March
sunflower	sow inside in March, plant out May–June; sow outside in April
sweet cicely	sow in spring, divide in autumn
sweet pea	sow inside January–February, plant out April; sow outside March–April
sweet rocket	plant March–April or in October
sweet sultan	sow in April
sweet william	(biennial) sow in May, plant out June–July; transplant September or following March
tansy	plant in spring or autumn
tarragon	plant March–April

thistle	plant spring or autumn. Self-seeding
thyme	plant in autumn; divide in spring
tobacco plant	sow indoors February–March, plant out end May–June
tomato	sow inside March–April, plant out end May–June
tulip	plant late summer–autumn
valerian	sow in April
verbena	plant March–April
viburnum	plant October–March
Virginian stock	sow May–July
wallflower	(biennial) sow in May, plant out in June, transplant in late summer–autumn
winter savory	plant in March–May
wintersweet	plant autumn–spring
wistaria	plant autumn–spring
witch hazel	plant autumn–spring
woodruff	plant in March

List 4: Months and what you might be doing in each

January

Inside
Go through	stores, throwing out anything rotten; catalogues, and make list
Find and go through	tins, boxes, bags, bottles where you might have stored seed from previous years
Buy	seed potatoes; put them to chit in the light indoors
Sow	eg antirrhinums, sweet peas
Take cuttings	from border chrysanthemum stools in store

Outside
Dig	adding humus and manure where appropriate, or, lime
Spike	lawn to improve drainage
Divide	edging plants
Plant	trees, bushes, bulbs and corms, eg currant bushes, roses
Prune	roses; cut down dead stems of straggly plants
Protect	new shoots from frost by covering
Manure	fruit bushes, rhubarb
Harvest	cabbage (Savoy, winter), celery, Jerusalem artichokes, kale, leeks, parsnips, spinach

February

Inside
Start	eg dahlias from stored or bought tubers, put seed potatoes to chit

Take cuttings	from border chrysanthemum stools in store
Sow	eg alyssum, antirrhinums, petunias, phlox, pinks, sweet peas, tobacco plants; cabbage (summer), leeks, lettuce

Outside

Dig	ground in preparation for planting shrubs
Prepare	onion bed, seed bed
Spike	lawn to improve drainage
Divide	edging plants, eg catmint, pinks; rhubarb
Plant	trees; hedges; deciduous flowering shrubs, eg cherry, *Daphne mezereum*, flowering currant, lilac; Michaelmas daisies; garlic, Jerusalem artichokes, shallots, rhubarb
Sow	eg beans (broad), cauliflowers, parsley, parsnips, peas
Prune	tips of summer-fruiting raspberries
Protect	new growth from frost
Feed	fruit bushes and trees
Dress	forget-me-nots, lilies, polyanthus, roses, sweet williams; strawberry bed
Harvest	cabbage (Savoy, winter), Jerusalem artichokes, kale, leeks, parsnips, spinach, sprouts

March

Inside

Take cuttings	of stools in store, eg border chrysanthemums, lupins
Sow	eg alyssum, asters (China), auricula, cowslips, petunias, phlox, pinks, primroses, stocks (Ten Week), sunflowers, tobacco plants; basil, beans

163

(French, runner), cabbage (summer), cauliflowers, celeriac, celery, courgettes, marrows, peppers, tomatoes

Outside

Dig	fork over soil lightly; manure where appropriate
Divide/plant	herbaceous perennials, eg phlox; lovage
Plant	eg clematis, lavender, Lenten roses, magnolia, Mexican orange blossom, pinks, rue, southernwood, sweet rocket, verbena, woodruff; summer-flowering corms and bulbs, eg acidanthera, lilies; chives, garlic, mint, onion sets, potatoes, rue, shallots, tarragon, winter savory; strawberries
Sow	eg candytuft, chrysanthemums, lupins, marigolds, mignonette, poached egg plants, poppies, sweet peas; beans (broad), cabbage, carrots, fennel, kohl-rabi, leeks, lettuce, parsnips, peas, radishes, spinach, turnips
Prune	roses
Thin	seedlings
Protect	shoots from slugs
Feed	irises, roses, fruit trees
Dress	roses
Mulch	strawberries
Harvest	cabbage (Savoy, spring, winter), cauliflowers, kale, leeks, spinach, sprouts

164

April

Inside

Sow

eg auricula, cowslips, petunias; beans (runner), courgettes, marrows, peppers, pumpkins, sweetcorn, tomatoes

Outside

Plant

tree lupin; evergreen shrubs, eg heather, hyssop, magnolia, osmanthus, pyracantha; perennials eg day lilies, marvel of Peru, pansies, pinks, sweet rocket, verbena; cabbage (autumn), cauliflowers, onion sets, potatoes, tarragon, winter savory

Plant out

eg carnations, pansies, sweet peas, tobacco plants; cabbage (summer)

Sow

eg alyssum, asters (China), candytuft, chrysanthemums, cornflowers, grass, lupins, marigolds, mignonette, nasturtiums, osmanthus, poppies, stocks (night-scented), sunflowers, sweet peas, sweet sultan, valerian; bean (broad, French), beetroot, borage, broccoli, burnet, cabbage (Savoy, summer), carrots, cauliflowers, clary, coriander, dill, fennel, kale, lettuce, spinach (perpetual, summer), turnips

Prune

flowering shrubs; clip evergreens

Protect

against insect infestation, eg roses, fruit trees

Feed

lily-of-the-valley

Dress

strawberries

Mulch

newly-planted shrubs

Harvest

broccoli, cabbage (spring, winter), carrots, cauliflowers, lettuce, spinach

May

Inside
Sow   basil

Outside
Lift   tulip bulbs when leaves die down
Prepare   dahlia bed
Plant out   eg alyssum, antirrhinums, asters (China), auriculas, chrysanthemums, cowslips, dahlias, petunias, pinks, primroses, stock (Ten Week), sunflowers, tobacco plants; beans (French, runner), celeriac, celery, sprouts, sweetcorn, tomatoes
Sow   eg alyssum, stocks (night-scented), sweet williams, Virginian stocks, wallflowers; beans (French, runner), beetroot, cabbage (winter), carrots, cauliflowers (autumn, winter), courgettes, kale, kohl-rabi, lettuce, marrows, parsley, peas, pumpkins, radishes, spinach, sweetcorn
Plant   eg pansies, pyracantha; winter savory
Thin   seedlings; pinch out broad bean tips
Protect   earth-up emerging potato plants by covering with soil; dust strawberry plants; spray fruit trees
Mulch   beans (broad)
Dress   strawberries, then mulch
Harvest   beans (broad), broccoli, cabbage (spring), carrots, cauliflowers, lettuce, radishes, spinach

June

Inside

Sow   stocks (Brompton)

Outside

Lift   tulips when foliage dry

Take cuttings/layer   carnations, pinks

Plant out   eg alyssum, asters (China), auricula, cowslips, dahlias, petunias, phlox, pinks, primroses, sunflowers, sweet williams, tobacco plants, wallflowers; basil, beans (runner), cabbage (Savoy, spring), celery, courgettes, kale, leeks, marrows, pumpkins, sprouts, tomatoes

Sow   forget-me-nots, stocks (night-scented), Virginian stock; beans (French, runner), beetroot, carrots, cauliflowers, kohl-rabi, lettuce, marrows, peas, radishes, spinach, swede, turnips

Plant   eg cherry pie

Prune   early-blooming shrubs, eg lilac, mock orange; pinch out strawberry runners, tomato side-shoots

Thin   beetroot, carrots, lettuce, parsnips

Protect   spray roses against greenfly; spray maincrop potatoes against blight; earth up potatoes

Feed   fruit trees, mulch roses

Harvest   beans (broad, French), beetroot, cabbage (spring, summer) cauliflowers (summer), carrots, kohl-rabi, lettuce, peas, radishes, spinach, turnips; gooseberries, strawberries

July

Inside
Sow   stocks (Brompton)

Outside

Lift and divide	irises
Plant	eg autumn crocuses, irises
Plant out	eg sweet williams; broccoli, cabbage (Savoy, winter), cauliflowers, kale, leeks, sprouts
Sow	forget-me-nots, stocks (night-scented), Virginian stocks; cabbage (spring), carrots, kohl-rabi, lettuce, peas, radishes, spinach, swede
Prune	cut out fruited raspberry canes; pinch out side shoots of tomatoes
Take cuttings	of rambler roses, or layer; layer strawberry runners
Protect	spray roses; earth up potatoes; spray tomatoes against blight
Feed	tomatoes
Harvest	beans (broad, French, runners), beetroot, cabbage (spring, summer), carrots, cauliflowers courgettes, cucumbers, kohl-rabi, lettuce, marrows, spring onions, peas, potatoes, radishes, spinach, shallots, turnips; currants, gooseberries, raspberries, strawberries

August

Outside

Dig	holes for planting shrubs in autumn; vacant ground, and manure where appropriate
Lift	onions, shallots

Plant	autumn crocuses, crocuses, lilies, snowdrops, tulips; strawberry plants
Plant out	broccoli, cabbages (Savoy, winter), cauliflowers, kale
Sow	marigolds; cabbage (spring), fennel, lettuce, parsley, radishes, spinach (winter)
Layer	strawberry plants
Prune	rambler roses after flowering; climbers; pinch out main growing shoots of marrow, tomatoes
Protect	spray chrysanthemums; spray gooseberries against mildew
Harvest	beans (broad, French, runners), beetroot, cabbage (summer). cauliflowers, courgettes, kohl-rabi, lettuce, marrows, onions, peas, peppers, potatoes, radishes, shallots, sweetcorn, tomatoes, turnips

September

Inside

Plant	bulbs for Christmas flowering, eg hyacinths
Store	beetroot, carrots, celeriac, marrows, onions, potatoes, turnips

Outside

Dig	trench for sweet peas, and peas
Plant	eg box, lavender. osmanthus, pyracantha; bulbs and corms of shade-loving plants, eg daffodils, fritillaries, irises, snowdrops; bay
Divide	bedding plants after flowering, eg polyanthus, primroses
Plant out	eg evening primroses, honesty, stocks

	(Brompton), sweet williams, wallflowers; cabbages (spring)
Sow	grass; eg dill, lettuce
Prune	currants, raspberries; cut down mint
Protect	celery by earthing up
Feed	tomatoes
Dress	lawn
Harvest	beans (French, runner), beetroot, cabbage (summer), carrots, cauliflowers, celery, courgettes, kohl-rabi, lettuce, marrows, onions, peas, peppers, potatoes, pumpkins, radishes, spinach, swede, sweetcorn, tomatoes. turnips

October

Inside

Store	beetroot, carrots, marrows, potatoes

Outside

Clean up	ground and fork in manure or lime; make fresh compost heap
Prepare	sites for fruit trees and bushes
Divide	phlox; lovage
Plant	tree lupin; evergreens, eg box, heather, *Magnolia grandiflora*, osmanthus, pyracantha, southernwood, virburnums; bulbs and rhizomes, eg hyacinths, iris (bearded), May-flowering tulips; spring- and early summer-flowering plants, eg clematis, Lenten roses, Mexican orange blossom, pinks, sweet rocket
Plant out	honesty, stocks (Brompton); spring greens
Lift	chrysanthemums

Sow	peas
Prune	evergreen hedges; cut deadwood from trees before leaf-fall; gooseberries, some pears
Dress	soil with nutrient in preparation for re-planting perennials; spike lawns and fertilize
Harvest	beans (French, runner), beetroot, cabbage (summer), carrot, cauliflowers, celery, courgettes, Jerusalem artichokes, kohl-rabi, leeks, lettuce, marrows, onions, peas, peppers, potatoes, pumpkins, radishes, spinach, swedes, sweetcorn, tomatoes, turnips

November

Inside

Check	stores for rot
Store	runner bean roots

Outside

Dig	ground. Manure where appropriate
Take cuttings	of fruit bushes
Plant	trees, eg apple, pear; bushes, eg roses; currants, gooseberries, raspberries; Lenten roses; bulbs, eg garlic
Sow	beans (broad), peas
Prune	gooseberries
Dress	lily-of-the-valley bed; top-dress grass after cutting and spiking; mulch rhododendrons, and fruit trees after pruning
Harvest	cabbage (summer, winter), carrots, cauliflowers, celery, Jerusalem artichokes, leeks, parsnips, pumpkins, spinach, swedes, turnips

171

December

Inside
Store   bulbs; box up chrysanthemum stools

Outside
Prepare   trenches for late winter-early spring planting
                      and sowing
Dig   ground
Plant   deciduous shrubs, roses, trees
Prune   cut down stems of chrysanthemums, pinch out
                      wallflowers; apple trees; root-prune over-
                      vigorous fruit trees
Protect   fruit trees with tar-oil wash
Harvest   cabbage (Savoy, winter), celery, Jerusalem arti-
                      chokes, kale, leeks, parsnips, spinach, sprouts,
                      swedes, turnips tops

List 5: Roses

My list of roses is pared down and rather arbitrary. Not only are there thousands of roses cultivated for their perfume, but enough books on this flower, and records connected with it, to fill a library as big and legendary as the lost library of Alexandria. Gertrude Stein's remark 'a rose is a rose is a rose' was a brilliant linguistic perception, but it is not true. The rose has, since ancient times, always been more than a flower. When considering whether the power of the sense of smell to operate at such a deep level of our life comes from its wordlessness I have wondered whether a flower without scent could have held the central position in our imagination that the rose does. 'Everywhere found, nowhere discounted' has been truly said of it.

The categorising of roses is infinitely complicated and learning about roses and choosing them seems to the uninitiated like studying form with horses at the races. The genealogy, breeding and naming of roses is not dissimilar in its arcane speciality. It, too, is governed by an international authority – the World Federation of Rose Societies.

I have divided the following list which contains just a few samples out of thousands, according to behaviour of growth. For me, the main division is between those that stay still (bush, shrub and bedding roses) and those that move (climbers and ramblers) with hedge roses somewhere in between. In the bedding and shrub category, therefore, you will find Gallicas, Albas, Musks and modern Hybrid Teas. You will find roses famous from the 16th century, favourites of the Victorians, roses popular in the 1930s, and delicious new ones bred by rose-growers today.

You can find out more about a particular rose and where it has come from in a good plant encyclopaedia. You may find a few inconsistencies, even between the experts: some shrub roses with a vigorous arching habit of growth may be treated as climbers (eg Cornelia). Some 'climbers' in one list may be under 'ramblers' in another. There are some shrub roses that have a climbing variety under the same name.

My attempt to give a colour description to each rose is a crude one. You must go to an illustrated catalogue or a nursery, or better still a rose-lover's garden, to realize what a glorious and subtle range there is.

Of course, nothing but the rose itself will tell you what it smells like.

Bedding and shrub

Alba Maxima (White Rose of York) (white)	June–July
Alec's Red (red)	June–October
Amy Robsart (rose-pink)	June–July
Beauté (apricot orange)	June–July and September
Belle de Crécy (cerise-pink)	June
Blanc Double de Courbet (white)	June–October
Blanche Moreau (white)	June–July
Blessings (coral-pink)	June–July and September
Buff Beauty (apricot)	late June–July
Camaïeux (crimson)	late June–July
Céleste (shell-pink)	late June–July
Celsiana (bright pink)	late June–July
Cérise Bouquet (cerise-red)	June–October
Charles de Mills (maroon)	June
Comte de Chambord (pink)	June–September
Constance Spry (rose-pink)	June–July
Cornelia (coppery-apricot)	August–first frost
Cristata (pink)	June–July
Duke of Windsor (orange)	June–July and September
Ena Harkness (crimson)	June–October
Fantin-Latour (pink)	June–July
Felicia (silvery salmon-pink)	August–first frost

Fragrant Cloud (coral-red)	June–July and September
Fru Dagmar Hastrup (pink)	June–September
Fritz Nobis (coral-pink)	June–September
Frühlingsgold (cream-yellow)	May–June
Gallica (Red Rose of Lancaster) (Crimson)	June
Général Jacquemot (deep crimson)	June–October
Grand'mère Jenny (peach-yellow)	June–July and September
Great Maiden's Blush (pinkish-white)	June–July
John Hopper (candy-pink)	June–October
Josephine Bruce (crimson)	June–July and September
Kathleen Ferrier (deep pink)	June–September
Kathleen Harrop (crimson)	June–first frost
Königin von Dänemark (pink)	June–July
Lady Sylvia (soft pink)	June–July and September
La France (white)	June–October
La Reine Victoria (deep pink)	June–first frost
Lord Penzance (buff-finished pink)	June–July
Louise Odier (lilac-pink)	June–first frost
Macrantha Daisy Hill (pale pink)	June–September
Mme Hardy (white)	June–July
Mme Isaac Pereire (deep pink)	June–first frost
Mme Louis Laperriere (crimson)	June–October
Mme Pierre Oger (mother-of-pearl-pink)	June–first frost
Moonlight (cream-white)	August–first frost
Mousseline (syn. Alfred de Dalmas) (pale pink)	June–July
Mrs John Laing (soft pink)	June–October
Nuits de Young (maroon)	June–July
Old Blush China (pink)	May–first frost

175

Ophelia (silvery-pink)   June–October
Papa Meilland (dark crimson)   June–October
Peace (yellow-pink)   June–July and September
Penelope (pink-cream)   August–first frost
Prima Ballerina (deep pink)   June–October
Reine des Violettes (mauve)   June–October
Roseraie de l'Hay (magenta)   June–September
Semperflorens (the four-seasons rose)
  (red-pink)   May–first frost
Souvenir de la Malmaison (pink)   June–first frost
Super Star (vermilion)   June–October
Sutter's Gold (orange-red)   June–October
Tour de Malakoff (magenta)   June–July
Tuscany (purple)   June–July
Wendy Cussons (cerise)   June–October
Whisky Mac (amber)   June–October
William Lobb (magenta-lavender)   June–July
York and Lancaster (pink and white)   June–July

Floribundas

Allgold (bright yellow)   June–October
Apricot Nectar (apricot)   June–July and
                                                September–October
Arthur Bell (yellow-cream)   June–July and
                                                September–October
Chinatown (custard-yellow)   June–July and
                                                September–October
Dearest (salmon-pink)   June–July and
                                                September–October
Grüss an Aachen (pearl-white)   June–October

Iceberg (white)   June–July and
                                        September–October

Maigold (bronze-yellow)   May–July

Margaret Merril (milk-white)   June–July and
                                        September–October

Violet Carson (silvery-pink)   June–July and
                                        September–October

Climbers

Banks's Rose (white)   May–June

Bobbie James (white)   June–July

Breath of Life (pink-apricot)   June–September

Cécile Brunner (pale yellow-pink)   June–July and September

Climbing Lady Hillingdon
   (apricot-yellow)   June–September

Etoile de Hollande (dark red)   June–July

Gloire de Dijon (buff-apricot)   May–October

Golden Showers (golden yellow)   June–October

Mme Gregoire Staechelin (pink)   June–July

Kiftsgate (white)   June–July

New Dawn (shell-pink)   June–September

Rambling Rector (white)   June–July

Wedding Day (cream-white)   June–July

Zépherine Drouhin (cerise-pink)   June–October

Ramblers

Albéric Barbier (cream-white)   June–July

Albertine (pink)   June–July

François Juranville (salmon-pink)   June–July

Gerbe Rose (lilac pink)   June–July

Goldfinch (buff-yellow)   June–July

Wild hedge roses

Dog rose (*R. canina*) (white-pale pink) June
Scotch or burnet roses
  (*R. pimpinellifolia* syn
    R. spinosissima) (creamy white) May–June
Sweet briar or eglantine (*R. eglanteria*)
  (rose-pink) June–July

Roses with fragrant leaves

Incense rose (*R. primula*) (yellow) May
Sweet briar or eglantine (*R. eglanteria*)
  (rose-pink) June–July

Essay on Smell

There are words to convey to other people our experience of seeing, words for shapes and colours, measurements and substances. We can describe (write down) what we have seen, and also re-present it by a non-verbal visual simulacrum: maps, charts, pictures, models of buildings or machines, sculptures, photographs. Even a clock is a visual version of time. We might say to a child, 'Go and see what the time is.' Learning to tell the time is, for us, learning how to look at the clock, not feeling with all your body what stage the day has got to in its passage from dawn through noon to night. Writing and musical notation turns what is primarily heard into a visual experience.

But who can map smell, who can give us fragrance with a few swift movements of a hand holding a pencil? Blind people can make out the shape of a person's face with their fingers, but someone suffering from anosmia cannot touch or hear or see smell.

It is much more difficult to describe what we smell than what our eyes register. We have not the words. What is to smell as red, blue, green are to colour? Nothing. Even with sight deficient in registering colour (apparently dogs and foxes see only in black and white, though goodness knows how anyone found that out), we can use words for shapes and place to indicate the look of a thing. What we see with even a colour-blind eye can be measured – three feet long; or delineated – square, triangular, round, curved; or placed – far, near, right, left. To convey sound we have precise notation that can be translated into words: the key of C major, minor, interval of a fifth.

It is true that much of the most effective description, even of sights and sounds, is carried out through comparison. Basically all words are metaphoric and stand for what they're talking about. The keystone to the art of language is simile. But if you want to convey smells through language there is no other way. There is no spectrum, no scale, no measurement whereby we can order our olfactory impressions. Alyssum smells of honey. Stocks have a clove smell. What do cloves smell of? Well, they are spicy, of course, but what is the smell of spice? It might be cinnamon or ginger and, if it is clove, it will smell of stocks. So stocks smell of stocks! – a sweet and virtuous circle but a limitation nonetheless.

If we want to be more precise, we may go away from our immediate olfactory reaction to, say, the smell of lupins on a hot June afternoon. 'It takes me back to a farmhouse where we used to be taken for holidays as children', we might say. 'The garden there smelt of that', or 'Wet evenings when my father's neck ached, and my mother cooked him slippery elm, peonies remind me of that'. It's more precise for us: interesting, perhaps, but no good to someone who has led a life that did not include lupins, a father with fibrositis, holidays in the Mendips, or the fact that it was a wet May when a child first heard the name of the gorgeous washed-out blooms that mingled with the steam from a pan on the stove.

The paucity of words whereby we can directly distinguish scent, in the way that geometry can distinguish shape, may contribute to the small part that accounts of smell play in explanations of the nervous system and the senses. What is less talked about becomes less noticed. Smells are very entangled with our emotions, but we generally think less about smells than about what we notice with our eyes. Could the lack of language for smell contribute to this? What we see is subjective; it is determined by the inner eye and our personal experience of seeing over all the years we have been alive and looking. There are, however, ways of checking with other people's experience. Lacking words, there is little possibility for objectifying our world of smell.

When people do talk about smell it is therefore often individual, interesting and personal. Nearly everyone I've read or talked to about the sense of smell has mentioned the very restricted vocabulary we have for exact description and how we have really to describe something other than smell to give an impression at all. It is put very well by Roy Bedichek, who was a Texan countryman and writer, in his engaging book *The Sense of Smell*.[1]

> I say 'damp and woodsy' but there are many kinds of woods and at least a dozen different damps out of which come hundreds of different damp woodsy odours . . . The damp and woodsy odour embedded in my own experience, 'nasalised' whenever the word 'sycamore' occurs, is that pervading an almost dry creek lined with sycamores somewhere in central Texas, either in quiet dawn or windless night fall. Thus the 'odour of sycamore' is the 'odour of sycamore'.

The following extract from a letter I received bears this out, again showing that our responses to olfactory experience, and analyses of our responses, are very individual and come from deep below the surface of communication.

> I realize since you started talking about smells that I find it almost impossible to pin them down with accurate descriptions that would actually make someone else know the smell without smelling it. The descriptions of smells you sent were recognisable to me when I knew the smell, like alyssum, so that I knew the type of honey smell you meant which to me is a thin sweet high-pitched smell, unlike some honey smells which are thick and rounder. The other descriptions were nice to read and did evoke a sense of smell but were more diluted and it was the other senses that became more important, like what things looked like, and it was with those smells more important

to have the physical descriptions and the talk about the other senses. The less familiar the smell is, the more description it needs, and that I suppose will be different for everyone reading it.

Smells do give me impressions. I find them long or short, thin, thick, round, fat, deep or shallow, warm or cold, sharp or soft, pricking, spreading etc. I find they act differently as well. Some ooze, others waft, some are like fireworks and seem to shower pockets of smell, some linger and others are short-lived, some hurt your nose, others can be tasted, some I am very wary of and reluctant to breathe in, others I can't breathe deeply enough and want to eat the smell.

All this helps towards a description but still doesn't actually define the smell. These impressions could be templates for groups of smells but the whole thing about a smell is that although it is 'like . . .', what it actually is, is itself.

There are reasons for the elusiveness of smells, for their seeming variability and inconsistent production and behaviour, that are not to do with the limitations of language. They lie in the nature of smell itself.

Odour molecules move from their source in all directions, even when the air is still. Being heavier than the air that carries them, they will not generally mount like a balloon, but be much denser low down near the ground which is why an animal like the dog has its nose to the ground. A dog's main means for receiving and sorting information of the world is its sense of smell, as ours is sight. The elephant's flexible snout, its trunk, can sweep closely over the ground, picking up hundreds of olfactory messages which a giraffe, who perhaps depends more on sight, would miss.

There is a theory that the different stages of evolution in animals manifested themselves when a dominance of one sense over another as its main means of survival developed. Thus a fish's sense of smell is major, sight not being very useful in a glaucous and dark element, but when some water animals developed into land animals and breathed clear air, information through the eye became more possible and necessary. For animals who climb trees rather than creep along the ground, good sight is more useful than good smell. Birds' sight is best of all. When a bird of prey is so high up in the blue we cannot see it, it will detect a brief scuttle of a tiny vole through bushes on heathland literally miles down. There would be no smells that high up. It has been suggested that it was when humans stopped loping along on all fours, taking in the immense amount of olfactory activity in, on and just above the ground, and got up on their hind legs so that their noses and, more importantly, their eyes faced outwards towards the horizon, that there was a great development of that part of the brain concerned with seeing.

We have to accept that the dominant sense in humans is sight. There are far more cells in the brain dealing with sight than with any other sense. A great deal of research into the eye and the part of the brain that enables us to see has resulted in detailed knowledge of how sight works, and this is paralleled by the capacity of our language to describe what we see.

The area of the brain where the sense of smell has its seat is referred to as the 'primitive' brain and up to the present it has been the part least accessible to exploration by scientists.

The term 'primitive' does not mean that because, over thousands of years, our complex brain has developed from that first swelling lobe of the very simple creature, we don't still need the primitive one, as if it were an appendix or the stub of what was once our tail. It is still the first (prime) base of our functioning as human beings. It is thought to be an area that does not deal with 'reason' (or with which 'reason' does not deal), but with 'instinct' and the 'emotions'. It is perhaps important in how memory works, and some are exploring the idea that it may be the seat of consciousness itself.*

So much of our experience of the world comes to us through our senses of sight and hearing which were considered to be the channels of information that made 'rational man' a superior being to other forms of life. Having no language, these depended on the more 'instinctive' and 'animal' senses of touch and smell. Sometimes, indeed, they were referred to as the 'lower' or 'minor' senses and less is known about them. Accounts of smell and taste take up less space in books on the nervous system, the brain, the human body, physiology text books, encyclopaedias, the *Oxford Dictionary of the Mind*, the exhibitions in the Natural History Museum, than for the other senses. In an excellent book, *The Many Human Senses*[2] by Robert Froman, there are four chapters concerning the eye, seventeen pages over three chapters on hearing, six pages on taste, smell and touch, a seven-page chapter on smell, two chapters on touch, one on pain, one on 'obscure senses'. In a standard textbook[3] on the senses published nearly twenty years later, the first 239 pages deal with vision. There are 90 pages devoted to sound, and finally come the 'chemical senses' – 19 pages for smell, 17 for taste.

Our noses are still a necessary and fully functioning part of our proper being, part of our defence system and a channel for our awareness of the world we live in. It is the second oldest part of us (it was thought to have developed from touch) and, as Bedichek put it, 'as a somatic

*I put these terms in inverted commas because they are linguistic divisions and the separation of 'emotion' from 'rational thought' is a description of a human-made concept and not a provable physiological difference like that between, say, a vein and a muscle. The current interest in finding the seat of consciousness reminds me of the search, through the past few thousand years, for the site of the soul. It is just that it has become the province of the scientists instead of the theologians. Perhaps this is one of the borders that science and religion share.

character, the nose ante-dates by aeons the legs in evolutionary history'.

There was apparently olfactory apparatus in very early vertebrates, creeping creatures low in the scale of life: small swellings from which a brain developed evolutionary ages later. It is thought that since 'Nature' makes use of what is there for one purpose, to accommodate a new function, these swellings became adapted to the functions of memory and consciousness. They were already the operating site for the sense of smell and the means through which, almost entirely, such a form of life would receive information of the world outside it. I suppose this is why those working in the forefront of neurological research today and interested in memory and consciousness are turning their attention to the sense of smell.

Losing one's sense of smell – to be anosmic – is dangerous as well as a deprivation of pleasure. The experience was described for me by someone who was in that situation for ten years through polyps in her nose growing back in spite of operations to remove them.

It did not hit me like blindness but I gradually began to realize I could not smell the coffee filtering or the nice dinner cooking, fresh lemons and oranges, the gentle fragrance of lavender or clean sheets. Then there were the garden smells like fresh earth after rain, wall-flowers, lilies, jasmine, roses, honeysuckle, lemon balm. These I missed very much.

There were some smells I was glad *not* to notice, like chopped onions, bad drains, newly painted rooms, babies' soiled nappies, elderly ladies' clothes they had been unable to take to the cleaners.

Gas was a dangerous thing not to smell if a saucepan boiled over, also if fruit was burning in the pan and I was out of the room. After a few experiences I made a rule not to move out of the kitchen while things were cooking.

There have been attempts at classifying odours. Heinrich Henning, a German psychologist, tried to work out a system. In it there would be six basic types of smell: flowery, fruity, resinous, spicy, burnt and putrid. Other attempts proved similarly limited in their usefulness scientifically because the data could only be arranged according to personal olfactory experience. This differs even more widely from individual to individual than with the other senses. In the 1940s, biochemistry was among the most active fields for scientific work, and research into the chemistry of substances in relation to the 'odour sensations' they triggered went ahead. A testable theory of 'osmics', or a science of smell, began to be formulated. Even this depended on recognising the shape of some of the vapour molecules that are connected to odour and which are in every bit of air we breathe in. It has been calculated that in a cubic inch of air there are about 400 million billion molecules, the majority being nitrogen, oxygen, carbon dioxide and water vapour. By the 1950s, the bio-chemists were continuing research into the shape of some of these vapour molecules. One of them, J. E. Amoore, had decided on seven primary odours (an unconscious analogy to the spectrum?). His selection was: camphoraceous, musky, floral, peppermint, ether-like, pungent and putrid.

Two things work against being precise about smells, apart from a lack of ways of communicating them. One is that people's reaction to smells vary immensely, much more than to the stimuli from other senses, and this is perhaps both a cause and a result of there being no normal everyday way of monitoring, of measuring, people's experiences in relation to smell.

There is a quite widely felt social restraint on mentioning smell and a public attempt to influence our attitude to it. A huge industry thrives on our wish to be able to ignore smell. If you think of the amount of money and resources, and the working hours of thousands of people, taken up in dealing with something we don't like to acknowledge the presence of, it is a bit surprising.

Queen Eleanor refused to stay in Nottingham in 1257 because it smelt so awful. It wasn't until 1875 that an Act of Parliament defined bad smell as a 'nuisance' (harmful, from the French *nuire*, to hurt. This origin might help those trying to explain the difference between a noise and a sound). Members of the Houses of Parliament couldn't ignore smell or pretend it didn't exist because in Westminster they were sitting on top of the most awful stench from the river.

Over the past two decades scientists have made enormous advances in what we can learn of how the brain works. The development of new non-invasive tools for recording information from the living brain is extending what is possible for them to explore. They are turning their attention to areas which up to now have been largely the terrain of psychologists and philosophers.

In the 1970s and 1980s, the leading research into the sense of smell was being carried out by a team in the Psychology department of Warwick University in England, the Olfaction Research Group. The findings of its members (John Kinge, Michael Kirk-Smith, Steven Van Toller among others) tended to be published in journals of psychology and behaviour. New journals are now springing up reflecting the combination of what were previously treated as separate areas for scientific enquiry. It is increasingly accepted that knowledge in every field is necessary to understand how the brain works, because its capacity for simultaneous combinatory processes far outdoes anything we can conceive of analytically by using as analogies to the brain the machines we have made.

At present (2002), the main focus for research into the chemical senses seems to be on what are called the Food Sciences. In Europe, the Department of Bio-sciences at Nottingham University in England in co-operation with Firmenich S. A. in Switzerland leads this research. At the Nottingham department's Food and Agricultural Sciences section, headed by Professor Andy Taylor, they are developing techniques to analyse the information carried by our breath when we breathe out after eating food. They are exploring the possibility that the brain can distinguish between breathing in (orthonasal) and breathing out (retronasal) and sends different messages about the food we are sniffing preparatory to putting it in our mouths, and what we are already chewing.

In the United States, research at the Monell Chemical Senses Center in Philadelphia is exploring the linking of the senses of taste and olfaction in the brain, and the way the brain can react to activity of the senses even when we are unconscious of any sensation.

The techniques scientists develop (the 'how' of their work) are sometimes as fascinating as the findings (the 'what' of the exploration), and on occasion the most exciting thing for the scientist is what she or he finds out when they are really looking for something else.

In his paper 'The Language of Flavour: Learning and Memory'[4], given at the Oxford Symposium on Food and Drink held at St Anthony's College in 2000, Professor Tony Blake, referring to the ways in which the olfactory bulb can send information directly into the limbic system, describes the precision with which its 'vast array of detectors ... respond to specific molecules' and that all the detectors for one type out of thousands of different molecules 'appear to be "wired" into the same receptor cells within the brain'.

He then refers to one of those leaps of understanding that sometimes seem to occur as a side-effect of research into an apparently different field: in recent work on mapping the human gene system, it was found that 'the genetic coding which controls the construction of our olfactory bulb is the largest sequence of DNA in our genome'. Among the cells that replicate the fastest in our bodies are the ones that go on regenerating new olfactory receptors, so even in humans there is far more cellular activity in connection with the sense of smell than with the other senses, even though the area of the brain dealing with sight is larger.

Research into many aspects of the way the brain and the senses work is confirming that the brain is capable of simultaneously processing information received though all the sensory channels. We will be aware of only a fraction of this traffic, and only a few people consciously experience synaesthesia (these are the people for whom colours will have a particular smell, or who will taste music in their mouths). Nevertheless, the functioning of our sense of smell, whether we're conscious of it or not, has a continuous effect on us. It guides our reactions, forms our likes and dislikes, and influences our relationships. It is perhaps more subtly powerful when we are unconscious of its functioning.

Even if you are not aware of it, your sense of smell is operating all the time. Since we must breath to keep alive, we cannot give it a rest as we can give our eyes a rest by closing them. Old text books and modern garden 'makeover' consultants may alike suggest that the sense of smell is marginal compared to our visual sense in supplying information to the brain about the world, but its effect on us is widespread and at a very deep level, and it is what our thinking brain developed from.

[1] *The Sense of Smell* by Roy Bedichek (Michael Joseph Ltd, 1960)

[2] *The Many Human Senses* by Robert Froman (G. Bell & Sons Ltd, 1966)

[3] *The Senses* by Barlow and Molton (CUP Ltd, 1982)

[4] in *Food and the Memory* ed. Harlan Walker (Prospect Books 2001)

Author's note: I would like to thank Professor Blake very much, not only for sending me his paper and giving me permission to use it, but for discussing the material in this essay with me and indicating the current frontline in this exciting field of research. He is Vice-President for Food Science and Technology in the Corporate R&D division for Firmenich S. A. and Special Professor in the Department of Bio-sciences at Nottingham University.

Book List

Apart from the indispensable help of *The RHS A-Z Encyclopedia of Garden Plants* (Dorling Kindersley 1996, 1998), the following is a very small selection of the many publications that I found enjoyable and useful whilst writing this book:

Diane Ackerman: *A Natural History of the Senses* (Chapmans 1990)

Roy Bedichek: *The Sense of Smell* (Michael Joseph 1960)

Maureen & Bridget Boland: *Old Wives' Lore for Gardeners* (Bodley Head 1976)

J. H. Clark: *The Cottager's Kitchen, Fruit and Flower Gardens* (London: Milner & Sowerby)

A. Corbin: *Le Miasme et la Jonquille* (Paris 1982)

Robert Froman: *The Many Human Senses* (G. Bell & Sons 1969)

F. A. Hampton: *The Scent of Flowers and Leaves* (Dulau & Co 1925)

Hugh Johnson & Pat Miles: *The Mitchell Beazley Pocket Guide to Garden Plants* (Mitchell Beazley 1981)

Eleanour Sinclair Rohde: *The Scented Garden* (The Medici Society 1931, 1989)

D. Michael Stoddart: *The Scented Ape* (Cambridge University Press 1990)

Jane Taylor: *Fragrant Gardens* (Ward Lock 1987, 1991)

Percy Thrower: *Percy Thrower's Encyclopaedia of Gardening* (W. H. & L. Collingridge 1962)

Lyall Watson: *Jacobson's Organ* (Allen Lane 1999)

Louise Beebe Wilder: *The Fragrant Path* (Macmillan 1932, 1990)

S. F. Harvey Williams & John J. Wells: *A Herb-grower's Notebook* (South Western Consultants 1981)

Index to the Plants

in main text

Folios in **bold** indicate entries where information about the plant may be found

Index to Essay on Smell